Tasting
the Past

Tasting the Past

Recipes from the Second World War to the 1980s

JACQUI WOOD

Cover Illustration: Utro_na_more/iStockphoto

First published 2009, as part of *Tasting the Past: Recipes from the Stone Age to the Present*.

This edition published 2020

The History Press
97 St George's Place, Cheltenham,
Gloucestershire, GL50 3QB
www.thehistorypress.co.uk

British Library Cataloguing in Publication Data.
A catalogue record for this book is available from the British Library.

ISBN 978 0 7509 9387 6

Typesetting and origination by The History Press
Printed and bound in Great Britain by TJ Books Limited

MIX
Paper from
responsible sources
FSC® C013056

Contents

Introduction

BRITISH FOOD HAS been hard to categorise in the past compared to the very distinctive cuisines of countries such as Italy, France and Germany. This is because it is an amalgamation of all of them, in the same way that the English language (the only truly European language, by the way) is a combination of five European languages: Celtic, Latin, Saxon, Viking and Norman. Our cuisine, too, is a combination of the typical foods of those that once conquered Britain over a thousand years ago.

But Britain's assimilation of the foods of other cultures did not stop after the Norman Conquest. During the Medieval period, the spices brought from the Crusades by the Normans were used in almost every dish by those who could afford them. When Britain itself began to have colonies, the culinary embellishments to our diet began again. During the Elizabethan period, strange produce coming from the New World was also adopted with relish by our forbears.

The Civil War period introduced Puritan restrictions to our daily fare, making it against the law to eat a mince pie on Christmas Day because it was thought a decadent Papist tradition. The Georgians took on chocolate and coffee with gusto and even moulded their business transactions around the partaking of such beverages. But it was really not until the Victorian period – when it was said that the sun never set on the British Empire – that our diet became truly global in nature.

This book will attempt to trace the roots of these influences on our traditional British cuisine. We should be very proud that we have adopted so much of the world's tastes into our traditional diet, rather than being ashamed of a seemingly patchwork and non-descript culinary heritage, as some people have described it.

This book will also look at the recipes we commonly use today and see if they are as modern as we think they are, or whether they have very ancient roots. I hope to show – as we cover the different periods from prehistory to the post-war years right up until the 1970s – that our love affair with exotic foods is not as new a trend as some of us seem to think. I have also included some recipes that, although well used and loved throughout history, have now been completely abandoned, in the hope that a few may be revived.

This book will hopefully become a manual for those readers who want to put on a themed dinner party, providing a wide selection of recipes from each period in history. I have not included those recipes that I feel you would never want to make, as some historical cookbooks have done in the past. Instead,

I want you to taste these dishes and experience what it was really like to eat during those particular periods. No one, apart from the truly adventurous among you, is going to acquire a cow's udder from the butcher and stuff it as they did in the Medieval period, or stuff a fish's stomach with chopped cod's liver!

I will begin this book by describing how our metabolism changed during the Stone Age, when we began to consume one of the most common food groups today: dairy products. Each chapter will begin with a brief introduction to the foods of the period that I found particularly fascinating during my research, and each chapter will end with the traditional Christmas food of the period (Solstice Feast food for the Celts). If you want to celebrate your Christmas in a completely different way, why not try some homely 1940s recipes or some 1980s-style party vol-au-vents?

The origins of some of our modern dietary problems

One modern phenomenon of our diet-obsessed society is the Low Carbohydrate Diet. These particular diets are thought to stem from mankind's Hunter Gatherer period, and are now designed to help those of us who have overindulged to lose weight. If one looks at any 'primitive' culture today, like the Bushmen of the Kalahari, you never see anyone overweight. The Hunter Gatherer diet comprised primarily lots of meat and fish. This type of food, once caught or hunted, would satisfy a person's hunger for longer than a cereal- or vegetable-based diet. We have all indulged in those huge Chinese takeaway meals, packed full of all sorts of vegetables that leave us feeling stuffed initially, but an hour or two later we start to feel hungry again.

As the name signifies, the hunter also gathered to supplement his protein-rich diet and to add variety, although fruits and nuts would have been seasonal and most of the leaves and stems they ate were only available in the spring and summer months. To summarise, the first Stone Age diet was predominantly meat and fish with seasonal banquets of nuts, berries and vegetation. One of the few vegetables available all year round would have been seaweed, which was probably gathered at the same time that shellfish were collected from the mid shoreline. It is also true that the tastiest wild vegetables can still only be found on the shorelines of northern Europe, where most Hunter Gatherer camps are found in the archaeological digs. These tasty vegetables include such delights as Rock Samphire, Sea Beet and Sea Holly, all of which are mentioned in my previous book, *Prehistoric Cooking*.

There are, however, serious consequences today for a large percentage of the population due to the ingenuity of the first farmers. Today's generation of allergic or food intolerant people can trace the origins of their dietary problems to the culinary practices of a group of Stone Age farmers.

It has been suggested that these problems are a result of modern agricultural businessmen overproducing chemically distorted products in their desire to make it all look the same and have a long shelf life in the supermarkets. Yet one of the most common food intolerances today is wheat: a hybridised wild grass plant. To find the origins of our first attempts at hybridising plants, we have to go back to the Fertile Crescent in the Middle East 11,000 years ago, to a people known as the Natufians who gathered wild grains to make into bread. The Fertile Crescent derives its name from the abundance of not just edible wild grains and pulses, but also the ancestors of our modern domestic livestock. It was almost inevitable, therefore, that the first settlements and agricultural experiments would have begun in this particular region. The city of Jericho, which is thought to be one of the only places on the planet that has been continually occupied for 11,000 years, is where these early plant experiments started as they cross-pollinated the wild grasses of the region.

Once mankind went down the road of cultivating the land, rather than wandering over it and gathering from it, we had entered ourselves into a lifetime of drudgery tilling the earth. The term 'the daily grind' is usually associated with boring and repetitive jobs. This comes from a time when people in each settlement would have had to grind grain into flour between two stones for an hour or more each day just to produce their daily bread. Lots of bread was needed too to feed the people that had to work hard on the land to grow the grain, and so we began a cycle that has no end. So those of us that cannot tolerate the gluten-rich hybridised bread wheat of today can blame those people 11,000 years ago who started our first manipulation of what was natural.

The Low Carb Diet – which is predominantly meat, fish, cheese and cream – is called the 'Hunter Gatherer Diet', as mentioned previously. This description is not really accurate, though, as the hunter-gatherers did not eat any dairy products until they settled down and became farmers.

The first cultivation of cereal crops was co-dependent on the domestication of the wild bull (the auroch). These were needed to pull the primitive ploughs to cultivate the land in order to grow the crops in the first place. Large numbers of female animals were needed, and so there was always a good and constant working stock of these beasts of burden. As a consequence, there would have always been suckling calves in those settlements. It would only have taken one person to drink some of the gallons of milk those beasts produced for their calves every day to get us on the road to lactose intolerance today.

Milk is primarily designed by nature as a food for young creatures, not for adults. This group of farmers therefore began the modification of the human body to tolerate milk and milk products well into adulthood – so much so that it has became a very normal part of our northern European diet today. Those early agricultural pioneers also discovered how to make hard cheese, which was a good way to store milk protein during the winter months. 'How on earth did they discover that?' you might think.

As usual with most discoveries, it was all about circumstance and chance. The early farmers had not perfected making large ceramic pots, and so a lot of the equipment they used when they were wanderers was also used in their new settled homesteads. One piece of equipment was the calf's stomach, used to carry water and to store it in their homes. When people decided to drink milk, it was natural that they would store it in the same containers that they used for water. The calf's stomach, however, contains the enzyme rennet, with which we make our modern cheeses today. If milk was put into the calf's stomach and hung in a warm place, it would therefore turn into curds and whey, and here we have the beginnings of our worldwide cheese production.

By 4,000 bc, most of northern Europe was growing wheat and enjoying dairy products in some way or another. However, for some unknown reason this love of dairy products was only popular in northern Europe. If you draw a line across the top of present-day Italy and include Austria, Germany, France, Switzerland, Scandinavia and Britain, you can see those ancient 'butter border lands' today. These are the countries that still love butter with their daily bread, whereas Spain, southern Italy and a large percentage of the world's countries do not really have this tradition. The colonies, of course, took this fashion with them around the world, so there are butter-loving outposts everywhere on the globe, most notably in America. But vast areas of the planet are still lactose intolerant because they did not adapt their metabolism as the northern Europeans did so effectively during the Stone Age.

We tend to think today that the lactose intolerant person is someone whose body has rejected a good and wholesome foodstuff. It is, however, the other way round. The lactose intolerant person's body has reacquired the original human metabolism, and so it is actually those of us who still consume them with relish who are the ones with the real dietary problems, with our love of butter and cheese on our daily bread resulting in excessive weight gains.

Second World War

WARTIME SHORTAGES LED to the creation of the Ministry of Food, the Dig for Victory campaign and powdered eggs. Marguerite Patten was instructed to invent interesting and tasty recipes for British housewives with very restricted larders. The interesting thing was that, because it was a very restricted diet, some of the poorer people in Britain had never eaten so well! The state took control of their diets, rationing sugar (which was very hard to get) and fat, and forcing people to eat wholegrain bread – for many, this would have been a healthier diet than the one they were used to. To supplement their diets, people dug up their lawns and grew potatoes and cabbages in their flowerbeds, providing their own, very locally sourced vegetables.

Just to highlight the difference between the British and the Americans during the war, I will relate a fascinating story. The American troops stationed in Britain brought with them their favourite chocolate bar – the Hershey bar – as part of their rations. Chocolate bars were so important to the American soldiers that the American government had their food technicians adapt the bar so that it did not melt too easily when the troops went into the tropics during the war. Having government food scientists spend their time developing a chocolate bar that does not melt seems worlds apart from what was happening in Britain, as the Ministry of Food was trying its best to get the nation enthusiastic about dried eggs!

The Ministry of Food, with its seemingly endless leaflets on cooking for the Home Front, was designed to do three important things. Firstly, to keep the morale of the British people high by giving them a challenge in the kitchen, the challenge being to make relatively normal meals while handicapped by rationing. Secondly, it was to make the housewife feel as if she was in some way contributing to the war effort by being inventive in the kitchen. Thirdly, and most importantly, because the government did not know how long or how bad the food shortages were going to become, they needed to ensure that the health of the next generation did not suffer as a consequence. They were only too well aware of the problems that bad diet could have on the development of children from the depression of the 1930s. They knew that children's diets, whilst not exactly fun, should include all their nutritional requirements, and invented such cartoon characters as Potato Pete and Doctor Carrot in order to try and make it fun for the children to eat their vegetables. The character of Popeye had been used in much the same way during the 1930s to make spinach seem attractive to young children. Other posters showed a silhouetted child drinking from a mug and the backbone of the child was a bottle of milk. The caption read: 'Milk: the backbone of young Britain.'

So the efforts of the Ministry of Food during the war made the diet of the poorer people of Britain better than it had ever been before. Cheap loaves of unhealthy white bread were replaced by wholemeal bread, and sweet, stodgy and fatty puddings were taken out of the diet due to the short supply of sugar and fat. Some evacuee children, sent to the country from the inner cities, drank fresh milk on a regular basis for the first time in their lives.

At the same time, there were posters saying: 'A clear plate means a clear conscience.' This attitude to food continued well after the war and has not helped those of us trying to lose weight! My mother in the 1950s would constantly tell me about the starving children all over the world, and how I had to clean my plate or it would mean I was ungrateful for the food I was given. How, in hindsight, my eating all my food would really make a difference was ridiculous, but I still feel a sense of guilt if I throw any food away. I have resolved this problem now by keeping three hens that eat all the leftovers, thereby recycling my waste into fresh eggs!

One thing those wartime days could teach the cooks of today is the ingenious use of leftovers. All too often we go to the supermarket and buy all sorts of ingredients for the week's meals – usually for at least seven dinners in my case. In my mother's day, a good Sunday roast would make one or maybe two different leftover meals on Monday and Tuesday, thereby saving a considerable amount of money and resources. You will see that there are a lot of leftover recipes in this section which, in our times of credit crunch, might be useful to revive.

Before I list some of the recipes used in wartime Britain, I would like to list some recipes from my own mother's cookbook during the war. My father was an engineer in Denmark before the war. Just weeks before the war broke out in September 1939, he came home to Britain to marry my mother – his fiancée of seven years. They took their honeymoon in Denmark and my father had just gone back to work when the war broke out. They did not get out in time and were soon captured by the German soldiers. My mother was taken to an internment camp for British women and children in Jutland and my father, for some unknown reason, was moved around various camps in Europe throughout the war. So after just a few weeks of marriage, they were both separated and were prisoners of war for five years. My mother had access to Red Cross parcels but, looking at the recipes from her own handwritten book named *Cookery Book, Denmark 1942*, she seemed to have had more ingredients to hand that weren't so readily available in Britain at the time.

Even though this chapter is about British wartime food, I think the recipes of a small British group in Jutland, cooking in their prison camp during the war, still fit well into this section. I had been brought up with stories of 'the camp' at Store Grundet, Vejle by my mother. After her death, I had the opportunity to go to an archaeology conference in Denmark in 1995, and so I contacted a local historian and told him about my mother's wartime story. He arranged for me to visit the place where my mother had been a prisoner. It has been empty since the war, and was in the process of being renovated. I spent the afternoon matching up photographs of my mother with parts of the buildings and taking pictures of what it is like now. I had always been intrigued by pictures of my mother on a beach at the time and was told by the historian that if it was a nice day, the German soldiers would take the women and children to the beach for the day in a truck. They were just ordinary soldiers, and I remember my mother saying that they were always very considerate and kind to them. What I did not know, and what my mother never told me, was that when the SS found they were losing the war, they arrived in the village and told the solders to kill all the inmates of the camp. The soldiers refused to do this and fought the SS troopers off until the British troops came in to relieve them. It must have been a very scary time for my mother, which is why she probably never told me about it. It just goes to show that on both sides in the middle of a war, most people do what their conscience tells them is right, no matter what the consequences. The soldiers from my mother's camp had lived with them for five years and were not going to kill them just before they were about to go home.

Curry or Paprika Stew

1 onion

1 tbsp of curry powder or paprika

350 g meat

2 tbsp dripping

1 tbsp corn flour

Salt and pepper

450 g boiled potatoes

Method

1. Fry the onion in the dripping in a stewing pan.
2. Add the meat to the pan with the curry powder or paprika.
3. Mix the corn flour with some water and add to the water in the pan.
4. Cook until the meat is tender.
5. Add the salt and pepper and a little sauce if preferred (she does not state which kind of sauce, but I should imagine it might have been tomato sauce, as she lists it as an ingredient in another recipe).
6. Serve with boiled potatoes.

Hot Beetroot

450 g beetroot

The juice of 1 lemon

1 tbsp sugar

2 tsp salt

Method

1. Cook the peeled and diced beetroot until tender.
2. Add the lemon juice and sugar and serve hot as a vegetable.

Beef Pinwheels

450 g minced beef

6 tbsp breadcrumbs

400 g mashed potatoes

400 g peas

2 tbsp tomato juice (or tomato
sauce)

1 egg

1½ tsp salt

¼ tsp pepper

2 tbsp melted butter

Method

1. Mix together the beef, breadcrumbs, tomato juice or sauce, egg, salt and pepper.
2. Roll this out between two sheets of greaseproof paper to 6 in x 12 in, and ½ in thick.
3. Cover half with potatoes and half with peas.
4. Roll up and cut into 1 in-thick slices.
5. Brush with butter and bake for 12 minutes on each side until brown.

Tomato, Cheese and Rice Bake

2 hard-boiled eggs

400 g thinly sliced tomatoes

125 g grated cheddar cheese

300 ml of white sauce (made with
milk, corn flour, butter and salt
and pepper)

225 g cooked rice

1 tbsp curry powder

Method

1. Grease a dish and place a layer of the sliced tomatoes on the bottom.
2. Cover with sliced hard-boiled eggs.
3. Sprinkle on the curry powder and then half the cheese.
4. Spread over half the white sauce then top with the cooked rice.
5. Top with the rest of the sauce and the cheese.
6. Cover with a piece of greaseproof paper and bake in a moderate oven for 30 minutes.

Bacon and Potatoes

225 g bacon

450 g potatoes

50 g butter

1 tbsp flour

Method

1. Fry the bacon in the butter in a pan for 5 minutes (but don't brown it).
2. Cut the potatoes into very thin slices and cook in the pan, with the lid on, over a low heat until done, stirring every so often. Serve at once.

Brown Stew and Dumplings

225 g stewing beef

3 carrots

3 small onions

2 tomatoes

1 celery heart

1 tsp gravy browning

Salt and pepper

1 tbsp potato flour

For dumplings

125 g flour

1 large potato, grated

1 tsp baking powder

1 tsp salt

Method

1. Chop all the vegetables finely, add them to a pot of water and bring them to the boil, simmering until tender.
2. Thicken with potato flour and put in the gravy browning to improve the colour.
3. Mix the dumpling ingredients together and moisten with water.
4. Make balls the size of golf balls and drop them into the stew.
5. Cook with the lid on for another 30 minutes until they are done.

Lemon Fromage

2 eggs, separated

50 g sugar

The juice of 1 lemon

The peel of half a lemon

2 tsp powdered gelatine

Method

1. Mix the egg yolks and sugar well.
2. Melt the gelatine with a little hot water and mix with the lemon juice and rind.
3. Beat the egg whites until stiff and fold all the ingredients together. Leave to set.

Strawberry Pie

Pastry shell

250 g flour

75 g butter

¼ tsp baking powder

½ tsp salt

3 tbsp water

Filling

1 quart strawberries

300 ml water

3 tbsp corn flour

1 tsp lemon juice

300 ml sugar

300 ml whipped cream

Method

1. Mix the dry ingredients together until they are like fine breadcrumbs and bind with water to make pastry dough.
2. Line a pie dish with the dough, making a twisted pattern at the edges to keep the shape.
3. Prick with a fork and bake in a hot oven for 10 minutes.
4. Line the cooled pastry shell with the strawberries, reserving 1 cup of berries for the glaze.
5. Simmer the berries for the glaze in the water for 3–4 minutes and mix in the corn flour and sugar.
6. Simmer until clear and thickened, and add the lemon juice. Leave it to cool slightly.
7. Pour over the berries and chill thoroughly.
8. Decorate with a border of whipped cream.

Swiss Roll

2 eggs

50 g flour

50 g corn flour

125 g sugar

1 tsp baking powder

1 jar of jam

A pinch of salt

Method

1. Mix all the ingredients together (except the jam) and beat well.
2. Pour the mixture into a greaseproof paper-lined Swiss roll tin and bake in a hot oven for 10 minutes.
3. Turn out onto a sugared board.
4. Spread with jam and roll up quickly.
5. Trim the ends and sprinkle with more sugar.

Ministry of Food Recipes

Here are some recipes from the Ministry of Food leaflets distributed during the war:

Lamb Chop Hot Pot

This is a very economical meal, and very tasty too.

25 g lard or cooking fat

50 g chopped onions

4 lamb chops

450 g thinly sliced potatoes

225 g sliced carrots

225 g sliced turnip or swede

A pinch of mixed herbs

2 tsp salt

¼ tsp pepper

300 ml water or stock

225 g shredded cabbage

Method

1. Melt the fat and fry the onions and chops on both sides for about 5 minutes.
2. Lift out the chops and put in the mixed vegetables, herbs, salt and pepper and stock or water. Stir.
3. Put the chops back on top.
4. Cover the pan and simmer for 30 minutes.
5. Add the cabbage and cook for a further 10 minutes. Serve immediately.

Meat Curry

This is a very interesting curry and well worth trying. I really like it with the macaroni, as suggested in the recipe.

1 small onion

1 medium-sized eating apple

60 g dripping or lard

450 g beef or lamb

1½ tbsp curry powder

4 tbsp flour

½ tsp dry mustard

350 ml stock or water

1 tsp sugar

1 tbsp chutney

1 tbsp marmalade

1 tsp black treacle

2 tsp salt

Method

1. Chop the onion and apple and fry in the melted dripping.
2. Add the meat, cut into 1 inch cubes, and fry until browned.
3. Remove the meat from the pan and work in the curry powder, mustard and flour.
4. Cook for 2–3 minutes and add the liquid gradually. Bring to the boil, stirring all the time.
5. Add the sugar, chutney, marmalade, black treacle and salt.
6. Put the meat back in and simmer for 1–1½ hours, or until tender.
7. In place of rice, serve with macaroni, barley or potatoes.

Mince-in-the-hole

125 g minced meat (beef, pork or lamb)	
1 leek, finely chopped	
2 tsp mixed herbs	
1 tsp salt	
A pinch of pepper	
25 g cooking fat	
Batter	
125 g flour	
1–2 eggs	
½ tsp salt	
A pinch of pepper	
300 ml milk	

Method

1. Mix together with your hands the mince, leeks, herbs and seasoning.
2. Form into small balls.
3. Melt the fat in a baking try and add the meatballs. Put in the oven to brown.

4. Make the batter by mixing the flour, eggs, seasoning and milk together.
5. When the meatballs are brown, pour over the batter and return to the oven for 30 minutes until the batter is cooked and brown.

Hamburgers in Brown Sauce

This hamburger recipe is good and spicy, and quite unusual to our modern taste buds, being served in gravy instead of in a roll with lettuce.

Hamburgers

225 g minced beef

125 g stale bread (soaked and squeezed)

A pinch of herbs

2 tsp salt

¼ tsp pepper

¼ tsp English mustard

4 tsp Worcestershire sauce

2 tbsp finely chopped onion

1 egg (optional)

Sauce

50 g dripping

1 small onion, chopped

60 g flour

600 ml stock or water

Gravy browning

½ tsp salt

| ¼ tsp pepper |
| 1 tsp chutney |
| 1 tsp sugar |
| 2 tbsp diced carrots |
| 2 tbsp diced potato |

Method

1. Mix all the hamburger ingredients together and shape into 8 rounds.
2. Fry in a shallow pan until browned, but not cooked through.
3. Remove the hamburgers from the pan.
4. Fry the onion until brown, add the flour and mix well.
5. Add the liquid gradually, stirring all the time until the sauce boils.
6. Add the other ingredients and the hamburgers and cover. Simmer for 15–20 minutes.
7. Serve with potatoes.

Beef and Lettuce Salad and Mustard Sauce

Corned Beef was one food that everybody was provided with at least once or twice a month. It was very useful and could be made to go a very long way. Here are just a few recipes that use corned beef as a main ingredient, rather than eating it in a sandwich with English mustard as we do today.

4 tbsp flour

1 tbsp mustard powder

1 tsp salt

½ tsp pepper

300 ml water

1 tbsp finely chopped onion

1 tbsp vinegar

125 g corned beef (a small can is about 200 g, so you can see how little was used)

1 medium lettuce

A few radishes and cooked peas to garnish

Method

1. Mix the flour, mustard, salt and pepper to a smooth cream with a little of the water, and then add the onion.
2. Boil the rest of the water and pour on to the blended mustard powder. Return to the pan and bring it to the boil.
3. Boil gently for 5 minutes, and then beat in the vinegar and allow it to cool.
4. Flake the corned beef and shred the lettuce, and mix these ingredients with the cold sauce.
5. Line a bowl with the outside leaves of the lettuce and pile the filling into the centre.
6. Garnish with slices of radish and cooked peas.

Corned Beef Rissoles

125 g mashed potatoes

125 g corned beef

125 g brown breadcrumbs

1 medium onion, chopped finely

2 tbsp brown sauce (HP sauce)

A pinch of salt and pepper

Method

1. Flake the corned beef and mix with the other ingredients.
2. Form into small burger shapes and put onto a baking tray.
3. Bake in a moderate oven for 15 minutes until brown, and then serve hot with cooked greens.

These rissoles make a good cold lunch snack the next day too.

Corned Beef Hash

200 g corned beef (1 small tin)

400 g mashed potatoes

1 onion

30 g margarine

Salt and pepper

Milk to mix

Method

1. You will need a heavy saucepan and a wooden spatula. Fry the onion, finely chopped, in a little of the margarine.
2. In a bowl, break up the corned beef with a fork and mix well with the mashed potato. Add salt and pepper to taste.
3. When the onions are lightly browned, add the rest of the margarine and the potato mix and fry, stirring all the time.
4. As it starts to brown on the bottom of the pan, stir into the mixture and keep doing this until there is an even mix of browned potato through the hash.
5. Serve at once with brown sauce.

Ministry of Food Curried Corned Beef Balls

1 small tin corned beef

50 g breadcrumbs

2 tbsp sweet pickle

2 tsp curry powder

1 small leek or onion, chopped

1 tbsp gravy

Method

1. Chop the meat up finely and mix with all the other ingredients.
2. Form into four balls.
3. Roll in brown breadcrumbs and shallow fry in a pan until browned all over.
4. Serve hot with gravy or cold with salad.

Macaroni Cheese

Here is an all-time favourite comfort food. This particular recipe is also from the Ministry of Food.

125 g macaroni
3 tbsp flour
300 ml milk
150 ml macaroni water
½ tsp English mustard (not powder)
¼ tsp pepper
125 g grated cheddar cheese (mature is best)

Method

1. Cook the macaroni in boiling salted water until tender for about 20–30 minutes.
2. Drain well. Retain 150 ml of the water and keep the macaroni hot.
3. Blend the flour with a little of the cold milk
4. Boil the rest of the milk and macaroni water, and then pour onto the blended flour.
5. Return the mixture to the pan, stirring all the time, and boil gently for 5 minutes.
6. Add the seasoning and two thirds of the cheese and the cooked macaroni.
7. Mix well and put into a greased pie dish. Sprinkle on the remaining cheese.
8. Brown under the grill and serve at once.

Creamed Sardine Pie

3 tbsp flour
300 ml milk
1 tsp salt
A pinch of pepper
A pinch of nutmeg
1 tsp vinegar
1 can sardines in oil
150 g short crust pastry

Method

1. Blend the flour with the milk and bring to the boil, stirring all the time. Simmer for 5 minutes.
2. Add the seasoning, nutmeg and vinegar.
3. Mix in the mashed sardines with the oil.
4. Line a 6 in flan ring with pastry and add the mixture. Cover with the remaining pastry.
5. Brush the top with milk and bake in a hot oven for 30 minutes.
6. Serve hot or cold with a green salad.

Fish Cakes

225 g cooked fish (any kind)
225 g mashed potato
1 onion, finely chopped
1 tbsp chopped parsley
A few drops of vinegar
1 egg (fresh or dried and reconstituted)
Breadcrumbs

Method

1. Flake the fish finely and check there are no bones.
2. Mix all the ingredients together, apart from the egg and breadcrumbs.
3. Form into fish cakes and dip in beaten egg and breadcrumbs.
4. Shallow fry the fish cakes on both sides until brown. These can be eaten hot or cold with salad or cold in a sandwich for lunch.

Fish Curry

1 small onion

1 small carrot

25 g lard

1 tbsp curry powder

3 tbsp flour

600 ml water or stock

1 tbsp vinegar

1 tbsp chutney

2 tbsp sultanas

1–2 tsp salt

350 g cooked fish

Method

1. Fry the onion and carrot in the fat until tender.
2. Add the curry powder and flour and cook for 1 minute.
3. Add the stock or water and bring to the boil, stirring all the time.
4. Boil gently for 10 minutes, and then add the vinegar, chutney, sultanas, salt and fish.
5. Heat through thoroughly for 5 minutes and serve with mashed potatoes.

Fish Pasties

225 g cooked fish (flaked)	
225 g mixed cooked vegetables	
1 tbsp vinegar	
2 tbsp chopped parsley	
150 ml white sauce	
¼ tsp pepper	
150 g short crust pastry	

Method

1. Mix together the fish, vegetables, vinegar, parsley, sauce and seasoning.
2. Roll out the pastry thinly into rounds about 6 in in diameter.
3. Place a portion of the mixture on one half and dampen the edges.
4. Fold the pastry over and crimp the edges to seal the pasties.
5. Bake in a moderate oven for 30 minutes.

These are very good hot or cold for lunch with a salad the next day.

Pilchard Pie

350 g tin of pilchards in tomato sauce
2 tbsp chopped parsley
2 tbsp chopped onion
50 g mashed potatoes
1 tsp salt
¼ tsp pepper
150 g short crust pastry

Method

1. Mash the pilchards well and mix with the rest of the ingredients.
2. Line a pie dish with the pastry and put in the filling.
3. Cover with the rest of the pastry.
4. Bake in a hot oven for 30 minutes.

This is very good cold with tomato sauce or chutney.

Potato and Bacon Cakes

450 g potatoes, cooked

6 tbsp chopped onion

75 g bacon

2 tsp Marmite or Bovril

1 tsp salt

A pinch of pepper

Milk and breadcrumbs for coating

Method

1. Mash the potatoes while still hot and chop the bacon.
2. Fry the bacon and then the onion until they are both brown.
3. Add to the mashed potato with the extract and seasoning.
4. Mix well and form into 8 cakes.
5. Coat in milk and breadcrumbs and bake in a moderately hot oven until firm for about 15 minutes.

Savoury Potato Biscuits

50 g margarine

75 g plain flour

75 g mashed potatoes

6 tbsp grated cheese

1½ tsp salt

A pinch of pepper

Method

1. Rub the margarine into the flour and add the other ingredients. Work into a stiff dough.
2. Roll out thinly and cut into shapes. Bake in a moderate oven for 15–20 minutes.

This mixture makes 24 biscuits.

Cheese Pudding

2 eggs

300 ml milk

75 g grated cheese

1 teacup full of breadcrumbs

1 tsp mustard

Salt and pepper

Method

1. Beat the eggs.
2. Boil the milk and stir in the breadcrumbs. Then remove from the heat.
3. Add the cheese, salt and pepper, mustard and beaten eggs.
4. Pour into a dish and bake for 30 minutes until set and brown.

Potato Puffs

450 g cooked mashed potatoes

Salt and pepper

A little flour

Filling

150 g sausage meat (or cooked root vegetables with 25 g grated cheese)

Method

1. Mix cold mashed potatoes with seasoning.
2. Add enough flour to bind the potatoes into dough.
3. Roll out the dough and cut into large rounds.
4. Put a little of the filling on one side of the rounds, dampen the edges and fold over.
5. Bake in a hot oven for 30 minutes.

Dresden Patties

I do not know the connection between Dresden and this recipe. It was devised, however, at a time when fried bread was a normal part of the British diet. Worth trying if you are partial to fried bread!

25 g dripping

50 g flour

150 ml stock or vegetable water

225 g cooked meat, chopped finely (or half meat and half cooked vegetables)

1 tsp salt

½ tsp pepper

1 tsp Worcestershire sauce

4 rounds of bread cut 2½ cm thick

Chopped parsley

Method

1. Heat the dripping and add the flour. Cook until slightly browned.
2. Gradually stir in the liquid and bring to the boil. Cook for 5 minutes.
3. Add the meat or mixture of meat and vegetables.
4. Cut a round into each slice of bread, and cut a smaller round in the middle of each.
5. Fry the rounds and inner circles in hot fat until golden brown.
6. Lay the large rounds in a dish and fill each with the meat and sauce
7. Put the small circle of fried bread on top of the sauce to form a lid, and serve with chopped parsley.

Woolton Pie

This recipe was created by the chef of the Savoy Hotel and named after Lord Woolton, the Head of the Ministry of Food at the time.

450 g diced potatoes

450 g cauliflower

450 g diced carrots

450 g diced swede

3 spring onions

1 tsp vegetable extract (or Marmite)

1 tbsp oatmeal

A handful of chopped parsley

Wholemeal pastry made with 150 g brown flour, 50 g margarine and ½ tsp salt

Method

1. Cook the vegetables with just enough water to cover, stirring to prevent it sticking to the pan.
2. Spoon into a pie dish and sprinkle with the chopped parsley.
3. Cover with a crust of wholemeal pastry.
4. Bake in a moderate oven until the pastry is cooked and serve hot with gravy.

Sausage and Sultana Casserole

450 g sausages

1 large onion, chopped

50 g sultanas

1 cooking apple, chopped

A pinch of dried mixed herbs

300 ml stock

Salt

Method

1. Fry the sausages and leave on a plate to one side.
2. Fry the onion in the sausage fat.
3. Put the sausages back in the pan and cover with stock.
4. Add the apple, sultanas, herbs and salt. Stir well.
5. Put in a casserole dish and cook in a slow oven for 1 hour.

Vegetable Pie with Cheese and Oatmeal Crust

700 g cooked mixed vegetables

2 tbsp coarsely chopped parsley

300 ml stock or water

For the crust

50 g oatmeal

50 g mashed potato

50 g grated cheese

100 g flour

25 g lard or margarine

Salt

Method

1. Place cooked vegetables in a pie dish and sprinkle with the coarsely chopped parsley.
2. Add the stock or water and seasoning.
3. To make the crust, cream the fat and potato together.
4. Add to it the cheese, oatmeal, flour and salt and combine it all together.
5. Add a little water if it is too dry – it should be a stiff dough.
6. Roll out the crust to cover the pie dish and put it on top.
7. Bake in a moderate oven for 30 minutes and serve with greens and baked potatoes.

Vegetable Broth with Sausage Dumplings

125 g self-raising flour (or plain flour and 2 tsp baking powder)
1 tsp salt
25 g suet
1 tbsp chopped parsley
125 g sausage meat
Water to mix for broth
225 g carrots
75 g turnips
75 g onions or leeks
125 g chopped outer leaves of a cabbage
225 g potatoes
1 litre stock (chicken if you have it)

Method

1. Chop the onions/leeks, carrots, turnip, cabbage and potatoes into small pieces and put in the boiling stock. Simmer for 30 minutes.
2. Make dumplings by mixing together all the remaining ingredients.
3. Mix with cold water to a stiff consistency and divide into 8 pieces.
4. Roll each piece into balls and dip in flour.
5. After the soup has simmered for 30 minutes, bring it back to the boil and drop in the dumplings.
6. Put the lid on the pan and simmer for 20 minutes until they are cooked.

Baked Fruit Pudding

This is a very hearty and at the same time cheap meal to make – great on a cold winter's day.

600 g stewed fruit of any kind
(apple and blackberries are good
for this recipe)

125 g stale bread

3 tbsp milk

2 tbsp sugar

Method

1. Put the fruit in an ovenproof dish.
2. Cut the bread neatly into cubes and cover the fruit with it.
3. Sprinkle the bread with the milk and then sprinkle over the sugar.
4. Bake in a hot oven for 20–30 minutes or until the bread crust is golden.

Raspberry Buns

225 g self-raising flour

A pinch of salt

75 g margarine

50 g sugar

1 tsp vanilla essence

150 ml milk (or milk and water)

2 tbsp raspberry jam

Method

1. Rub the margarine into the flour and add the sugar.
2. Mix to a stiff dough with the water and the vanilla essence.
3. Cut the dough into 12 pieces and form into buns. Make a hole in the middle of each.
4. Put a little of the raspberry jam in the holes and pull the dough over it to seal in the jam.
5. Roll lightly in sugar and bake in a hot oven for 10 minutes or until firm to the touch.

Wait until they cool before trying them, as the jam inside will be very hot!

ANZAC Biscuits

ANZAC is an acronym for Australian and New Zealand Army Corps, which was formed in the First World War. ANZAC biscuits are also known as soldier biscuits. This recipe is from Ministry of Food Leaflet 38, and probably intended to show a certain solidarity with the Australian and New Zealand troops in the Second World War.

75 g margarine
75 g sugar
1 tbsp syrup
½ tsp vanilla essence
1 tsp bicarbonate of soda
2 tbsp hot water
75 g flour
225 g rolled oats

Method

1. Cream the margarine and sugar together and add the syrup and vanilla essence.
2. Mix the bicarbonate of soda and the water together and add to the margarine and sugar mixture.
3. Add the rest of the ingredients and make a stiff dough.
4. Place a teaspoon at a time of the mixture 2in apart on a baking tray and cook for 20 minutes in a moderate oven.

This recipe makes 36 biscuits.

Wartime Christmas

Mock Goose (Country Style)

There are lots of references in the wartime literature to mock goose being served at Christmas, but most of the recipes just seem to be layers of onions and potatoes in a dish topped with cheese – not at all goose-like in my opinion! Here is a recipe from the countryside for mock goose, which was a bit more like the real thing.

1 bullock's heart

2 bay leaves

4 cloves

2 meat stock cubes

4 large onions

1 tbsp corn flour

8 sage leaves

125 g suet or fatty bacon

225 g breadcrumbs

1 egg

Salt and pepper

Dripping
Baked potatoes to serve

Method

1. Wash the heart and put in a pan with enough water to cover it.
2. Add pepper, salt, bay leaves, cloves and meat cubes.
3. Simmer gently for 4–5 hours until tender.
4. Put to one side until the next day.
5. Take the fat off the stock in the pan and mix together with the egg, chopped onions, chopped sage leaves, suet/bacon and breadcrumbs.
6. Make into forcemeat balls, leaving a little of the mixture to stuff the heart.
7. Put the stuffed heart in a baking tin, suround with the forcemeat balls and cover with dripping.
8. Bake in a hot oven for 30 minutes.
9. Strain the stock in which the heart was boiled and use about 600 ml for the gravy.
10. Thicken the stock with corn flour and serve with the heart and baked potatoes.

The leftover heart can be minced the next day and mixed with the gravy to make another dinner. The rest of the stock makes an excellent soup when you add all kinds of vegetables to it.

Savoury Sprouts

225 g sprouts

1½ tbsp flour

150 ml vegetable water and milk mixed

3 tbsp grated cheese

A few drops of lemon essence

½ tsp salt

A pinch of pepper

Method

1. Boil the sprouts in salted water. Keep hot and reserve the liquid.
2. Blend the flour in a little of the liquid and bring the remainder to the boil, stirring all the time. Add the blended flour.
3. Simmer for 5 minutes until thickened and add the cheese, lemon essence and more seasoning if needed.
4. Add the sprouts and reheat. Serve very hot with the mock goose and baked potatoes.

Ministry of Food Christmas Pudding Recipe (A Good Dark Christmas Pudding)

500 g plain flour

½ level tsp baking powder

½ level tsp nutmeg

¼ tsp salt

½ tsp cinnamon

1 tsp mixed spice

50 g suet or fat

75 g sugar

225–450 g mixed dried fruit

125 g breadcrumbs

25 g marmalade

1 egg

150 ml brandy, rum, ale, stout or milk

Method

1. Sift the flour, baking powder, salt and spices together.
2. Add the sugar, fruit, breadcrumbs and suet.
3. Mix with the marmalade, eggs and liquid and beat thoroughly.
4. Put into a greased basin, cover with greaseproof paper and steam for 4 hours.
5. Remove the paper and cover with a piece of cloth. Store in a cool, dry place.
6. Steam on Christmas Day for 2–3 hours before serving.

Christmas Cake (Without Eggs)

100 g grated carrots

3 tbsp golden syrup

125 g margarine

1 tsp bicarbonate of soda

½ tsp almond essence

½ tsp vanilla essence

160 g mixed dried fruit

300 g flour

1 tsp cinnamon

1 small teacup of black tea, hot

Method

1. Pour the tea over the dried fruit and leave overnight.
2. Cream the golden syrup and margarine together.
3. Beat in the carrots, the bicarbonate of soda, the essences and spices.
4. Mix in the dried fruit (it will have absorbed most of the tea by now) and then stir in the flour.
5. Line a cake tin with greaseproof paper and add the cake mix to it, spreading it out evenly.
6. Pre-heat the oven to hot and then put the cake in. Turn it down to cool and bake for 3 hours or until firm to the touch.

Ministry Mock Icing for Christmas Cake

2 tbsp water
6 tbsp dried milk
4 level dessertspoons of sugar
Colouring and flavouring

Method

1. Heat the sugar and water gently until the sugar has dissolved.
2. Add the dried milk gradually, beating all the time.
3. Add colouring or flavouring (almond essence is nice).

For chocolate icing (for chocolate log) use 5 tbsp dried milk and 1 tbsp cocoa powder instead.

Ministry of Food Mincemeat

225 g mixed dried fruit

125 g apples

125 g sugar

125 g margarine or suet

½ tsp mixed spice

½ tsp cinnamon

1 tsp nutmeg

¼ tsp salt

6 tbsp of brandy, sherry, rum,
stout or ale

½ tsp lemon essence

2 tbsp marmalade

A few drops of rum essence (optional)

Method

1. Mince fruit and apples together or chop finely. Add all the other ingredients to the mix.
2. Put into small jars and tie down securely. Store in cool, dry place.

This will only last 10 days, so only make the amount you will need.

Mock Rum Cream for Mince Pies

2 tbsp custard powder

300 ml milk

25 g margarine

1 tbsp sugar

A few drops of rum essence

Method

1. Blend the custard powder with a little of the cold milk.
2. Warm the rest of the milk in a pan, add the warm milk to the powder paste and return to the pan.
3. Stir over a heat until cooked and thickened.
4. Let it go cold.
5. Cream the margarine and sugar together well. Beat into the cold custard gradually and add the rum essence.
6. Keep in a cool place and serve with hot mince pies.

Christmas Fruit Snow

300 ml water

1 tbsp sugar

1 level tbsp powdered gelatine

150 ml fruit pulp (made from
stewed or bottled fruit)

Method

1. Heat the water and sugar together, pour on the
   gelatine and stir until dissolved.
2. When cool, add the fruit pulp and beat until it is
   the consistency of whipped cream.
3. Serve in individual glasses or pile into a dish.

Crumb Fudge

At Christmas time, sweets for the children would have been scarce, but this recipe is well worth trying.

2 tbsp golden syrup
50 g margarine
50 g sugar
50 g cocoa
A few drops of vanilla essence
175 g dried breadcrumbs

Method

1. Heat the syrup, margarine, sugar and cocoa gently in a pan until melted.
2. Stir in flavouring and then the breadcrumbs.
3. Mix well and turn into a well greased sandwich tin.
4. Mark into fingers with a knife.
5. Leave for 24 hours, as it improves if kept for a day or two (if it lasts that long, that is!).

The Post War Years

WHEN QUEEN ELIZABETH II came to the throne in 1952, Britain was in a sorry financial state. There was still rationing of basics such as sugar, butter, margarine, cheese, cooking fat, bacon, meat and tea, which, as you can imagine, was a bit depressing for the homecoming troops who had been relatively well fed on forces' rations. But by 1954, rationing finally ended and, if you had the money, you could buy as much food as you wanted from the shops. Most people though, due to financial restraints, kept to a very similar diet to the one they had had during the war.

In 1955, the first commercial TV station was launched and suddenly all sorts of products were advertised with catchy slogans, such as the Egg Marketing Board's 'Go to work on an Egg'. New sugar-laden breakfast cereals were also promoted with cartoon characters, such as the Snap, Crackle and Pop trio created to advertise Rice Krispies.

Things got back to some sort of normality in the high streets by the late 1950s, and rationing was more or less forgotten. I used to go to the local shops for my mother at that time, and had to tell the man how thickly we wanted our bacon sliced. The butter was cut from a block out of a barrel from Kiel, and cheese was sliced to order with a wire. Everything was wrapped in greaseproof paper or put in a brown paper bag, and apart from tinned food, nothing was pre-packed. On my way home from school, I used to go into the grocer's and ask for a 1d bag of broken biscuits, as all biscuits were sold loose in glass-topped boxes around the shop. During those times, my father had a love of bilberry pie, so when they were in season I would go to the green grocer and ask for 2 lb of the berries, which were put into a brown paper bag. I had to run home quickly then, as the juices would start to seep through the paper and it would soon fall apart! The green grocer's shop was a wonderful, earthy smelling place too. The potatoes were loose and came out of a number of huge hoppers, depending on whether you wanted a floury or waxy variety, and fruits like strawberries and gooseberries were bought with relish when they came into their short seasons. The local shops included a newsagent's, a green grocer's, a baker's, a butcher's, a grocer's, an ironmonger's, a ladies' dress shop and a haberdasher, where you could choose socks and handkerchiefs from wooden drawers.

Then, in 1960, the ladies' dress shop on the corner was sold and in its place there opened a mini-market. This was very exciting for me at the time, as for the first time I was told to take a basket and pick items of food off the shelves for myself. Usually you never touched the food you were going to buy, as the assistants behind the counter would get everything for you. The mini-market was not a big shop, and the aisles between the shelves were quite small, but it was still an amazing novelty to us at the time. The food was all pre-packed and was much cheaper to buy, as it only required one person to take your money, rather than a number of assistants in a variety of small local shops.

The age of convenience had begun, and not long after that, self-service petrol stations began to be built. The number of local grocery stores fell from 150,000 in 1961 to just 60,00 by 1981. It was the beginning of the end for the small local shopkeeper with his personal service and local produce.

The 1960s marked the time of Ideal Home Exhibitions in Britain, where new foods could be sampled and amazing gadgets could be demonstrated. I remember going every year to the Ideal Home Exhibition with my mother and delighting in the endless free samples, from haggis to Mary Baker fudge frosting. Our bags were laden with little goodies to take home, and we spent hours watching demonstrations of new kitchen gadgets. After watching the demonstration, you would wonder how on earth you had ever managed in the kitchen without them. Once home, however, it was never more than a month before they ended up at the back of the cupboard collecting dust. It was a time of plenty, or so it seemed.

TV cooks became popular during those days, as people wanted to be shown how to change their cooking habits. Fanny Craddock was queen during this time, and she always wore evening dresses and frilly aprons on her show. She also ordered her husband Johnny about in her TV kitchen as she prepared just the thing for the formal dinner party. By the end of the decade, new types of TV cooks, like Graham Kerr, also known as 'The Galloping Gourmet', travelled the world showing more exotic foods in a very debonair way. He also used his unashamed sex appeal to capture large audiences.

People were just starting to take to the air and go to the Costa del Sol in Spain on package holidays, and so to be able to have some Spanish-style dried paella when you got home was a wonderful thought. There were lots of new instant meals that could provide that exotic flavour simply by pouring boiling water over them. Vesta was the most popular, with TV adverts showing people eating exotic foods from all over the world, before showing you the packet it had come from. Exotic meals like chow mein in a box was one, where you even made your own crispy noodles on top and sprinkled it all with little sachets of soy sauce. The foods were, of course, heavily laced with monosodium glutamate (msg), of which we were unaware at the time. All we knew was that they were incredibly tasty!

In 1961, a new technique for aerating bread to produce the standard sliced loaf was invented. It was called the Chorleywood process, and we were soon on the way to losing our local bakers, many of which were bought up by the huge industrial flour millers, who sold mainly their own large, white, sliced loaves. Companies like Bird's Eye, Ross and Findus started to produce a range of products for the new frozen food industry. Freezer sections of the mini-markets soon became full of fish fingers and frozen peas. No more podding peas from the green grocer's before the Sunday roast for me! We all thought it was wonderful, though. Everything was about labour saving and convenience. In 1974, the Smash adverts on TV for instant dried potato mash showed creatures from Mars laughing at the gardener for digging up his potatoes from the ground, peeling them, boiling them, then mashing with a potato masher. They suggested that anyone who did this was old fashioned and well behind the times.

I can't talk about convenience foods, however, without mentioning the OXO cube, and those cosy family scenes of the 1960s and '70s that portrayed the fun and banter of a typical family dinner. The adverts implied that if you did not sprinkle the magic ingredient – the OXO cube – onto your meal, the food would be tasteless and life in general would be boring. The first stock cube was actually invented by Baron Leibig, who devised a way to process pulped beef into a cube in 1865, although he was trying to produce a healthy concentrate of meat, and not striving to save the housewife time in the kitchen!

A typical convenience food menu we were taught to serve during domestic science classes at school was as follows: a starter of packet soup, followed by Vesta chow mein and finished with chocolate flavoured Angel Delight and tinned pears. This was, by the way, my school's way of trying to keep up with the times. We were also taught over two years all the basic cooking skills, which I feel would be of great benefit to re-introduce into the curriculum today, as most young people do not even know how to make simple pastry.

The 1960s, though, were all about the modern housewife having more time for leisure activities instead of being 'chained to the kitchen sink', as they used to say. Then the last straw was placed on the camel's back for our homely British food. The Wimpy bar arrived on our high streets, originally an American burger chain named after Popeye's gluttonous friend, Mr. J. Wellington Wimpy, who was always craving a hamburger. His catchphrase was, 'I'd gladly pay you Tuesday for a hamburger today.' The company that owned Lyon's Corner houses bought the Wimpy franchise, and we saw our first Wimpy bar in 1954 in London. It was not until the 1970s, however, that the franchise spread nationwide. The burgers were cooked when you ordered them and there were benders surrounding the burger (huge frankfurters). Oh, it was all so exciting at the time, and so American, just like in the movies! The first Wimpy restaurant in the West Country was opened on 27 July 1961. The countless franchise restaurants in the South West have all now gone, but the Penzance restaurant is still there, serving many of the meals it did in 1961!

The coming of the out-of-town supermarket and the home freezer suddenly made cooking all too easy and far too convenient. As you had gone out of your way to get to the supermarket, it seemed ridiculous not to get everything you needed for the whole week while you were there. Before the supermarkets came, you would decide what you wanted every day and go to get it from the local shops. The shopping trolley soon replaced the basket, as people were buying so much in one go. You had to imagine what you wanted every day in advance, and there were those displays of sticky doughnuts and ready-made meals that made it all so easy to slip into the habit of buying far too much food. The easy access to sugary pre-packaged foods has really led to our obesity problems today.

There were other influences on the British post war diet that came in the 1950s, with the first Caribbean immigrants arriving into Britain to fill the posts needed in the transport industry and the new health service. Yet their Caribbean food did not really take off during that time. It was not until the mid-1960s – when the Chinese immigrants from Hong Kong promoted their cuisine by setting up Chinese restaurants on every high street – that freshly made exotic foods were available in Britain. Then, in the 1970s, with the expulsion of Ugandan Asians by Uganda's President, Idi Amin, our old love of Indian food could be rekindled as Indian restaurants spread throughout all the major cities in Britain, competing, as they do now, with the Chinese restaurants for that Saturday night meal in town.

Here are some real post war recipes, perfect both for every day and for entertaining – just the thing for that retro party! Below is the classic special dinner party menu of the time.

The Original Prawn Cocktail

Everybody's favourite starter in the 1960s and 1970s.

1 lettuce
225 g shelled prawns
4 tbsp mayonnaise
4 tbsp tomato sauce
A dash of Worcestershire sauce
A pinch of cayenne pepper
Salt and pepper
Brown bread and butter with crusts taken off
4 lemon slices

Method

1. Shred the lettuce and pile into the bases of tall glasses.
2. Divide the prawns among the glasses, saving 4 heads for decoration (or just 4 prawns, if you have bought them ready peeled).
3. Mix the mayonnaise, tomato sauce, Worcestershire sauce, cayenne pepper, salt and pepper together.
4. Divide this between the glasses and pour over the top of the prawns.
5. Garnish each glass with a prawn and a slice of lemon and serve the glasses on saucers with brown bread and butter triangle slices.

Duck a l'Orange

2¼ kg duck

1 level tbsp flour

Coarsely grated rind and juice of 2
medium oranges

2 tbsp dry red wine

2 tbsp redcurrant jelly

½ wine glass of sherry

Seasoning to taste

Garnish

2 thinly sliced oranges

Watercress

Method

1. Put the chocolate in a heatproof bowl and add the milk. Place over a pan of simmering water to melt the chocolate.
2. Remove the bowl from the heat and beat in the butter, then the sugar. Continue to beat until the mixture becomes pale.
3. Beat in the flour and salt, and the egg yolks one at a time.
4. Beat the egg whites until stiff and gently fold into the mixture.
5. Butter a 20 cm loose-bottomed cake tin and put in a preheated hot oven for 40 minutes or until a skewer comes out clean when inserted in the cake.
6. Turn onto a wire rack and when cold, cut the cake into three layers.
7. Spread on the bottom layer half the jam or cherries.
8. Whip the cream lightly and spread a third of the cream over the cherries.
9. Repeat with the second layer and put the rest of the cream on top of the cake.
10. Pipe rosettes of cream around the top edge of the cake and place a preserved cherry on top of each rosette.
11. Sprinkle the grated chocolate over the cream in the centre.

Gaelic Coffee

The perfect finish to any special meal in the 1960s.

3 dessertspoons of whisky

1 level tbsp light brown sugar

Fresh strong coffee

Double cream

Method

1. Heat a stemmed wineglass with hot water and dry quickly (if you are not sure about the glass, find a thick one).
2. Pour the whiskey into the glass and stir in the sugar.
3. Pour in the coffee, leaving an inch below the rim, and keep stirring until the sugar has dissolved.
4. Pour the cream over the back of a teaspoon so that it floats on the surface to a depth of about an inch.

A must-have with the coffee is a dish of the new and very elegant After Eight Mints, as advertised on TV!

The Cocktail Party

The 1960s was the era of the themed party: coffee parties, tea parties, spaghetti parties, cheese and wine parties, buffet parties, pancake parties, fondue parties and, of course, the cocktail party for the more sophisticated gathering.

Dry Martini

Bond always had his with vodka, but gin was the original recipe.
1 part gin, 2 parts extra dry martini, crushed ice and decorated with a green olive.

White lady

2 parts gin, 1 part lemon juice and 1 part Cointreau, put into a cocktail shaker with crushed ice.

Daiquiri

2 parts Bacardi rum, 1 part lime juice, a dash of Angostura Bitters and ice.

Gin and Italian

Or, as my mother called it, Gin and It!
1 part gin, 2 parts sweet red vermouth and ice, topped with a maraschino cherry.

Gin and Tonic

You couldn't have a cocktail party without this one!
1 part gin, three parts tonic water, ice and a slice of lemon or lime.

Nibbles

Bowls of olives, crisps, cheese biscuits, cocktail onions and cocktail gherkins were served. Also popular was the classic melon, cut in half and covered in cocktail sticks with various nibbles attached: cheese and pineapple, cheese and cocktail onions, melon cube and prawns, melon and Parma ham, radish roses piped with cream cheese and small frankfurter sausages. Trays of little shapes of toasted bread were also served, with combinations of the following on top: prawns and mayonnaise, liver pate and rings of gherkin, smoked salmon and cream cheese, and hard-boiled egg slices with anchovy fillets curled on top. Trays of tiny sandwiches would also have been served, no more than 4 cm in diameter and, of course, the cream cheese and asparagus pinwheels were a must! These were made by cutting the crusts off white bread and rolling it so that it was very thin. The bread was then spread with butter, cream cheese and seasoning. Across one side of the bread was placed a line of tinned asparagus spears, and the whole thing was then rolled up before being sliced into rings.

The Fondue Party

Cheese Fondue

Another typical party of the 1960s was the fondue party. It originally became popular when people came back from winter sports holidays in Austria. A fondue set seemed to have been one of the most popular wedding presents at the time too, but I wonder how many people actually used them on a regular basis. This is the classic cheese fondue recipe, if you happen to have a set at home, or spot one at a local car boot sale!

450 g Gruyère cheese, grated

300 ml dry white wine

2 tsp corn flour (this prevents the cheese from curdling)

Seasoning

1 tbsp brandy

Method

1. Butter the bottom and sides of an earthenware casserole and add the cheese, seasoning and white wine mixed with the corn flour.
2. Heat slowly, stirring all the time, and add the brandy.
3. Transfer it into your fondue pot and light the candle underneath.
4. Offer your guests soft white bread cubes and toasted bread cubes to dunk.

It is actually very tasty, and still a fun way to enjoy an evening with friends.

The Buffet Party

Eggs Mimosa

Eggs mimosa was sometimes served as a starter, but it was also a good buffet dish. An alternative egg dish was curried eggs, which I absolutely love. I serve them at most buffet parties – the perfect excuse to make them! They are very 1950s, and apparently still incredibly popular in New Zealand.

4 hard-boiled eggs

125 g frozen prawns

300 ml mayonnaise

Watercress to garnish

Method

1. Slice the eggs lengthwise and take out the yolks.
2. Sieve two thirds of the egg yolk into a basin and with a folk add the prawns and a little of the mayonnaise to bind them together. Stir with a fork.
3. Spoon the mixture back into the egg whites and arrange on a dish. Cover with the remaining mayonnaise.
4. Sieve the remaining egg yolk over the eggs and serve with a watercress garnish.

Curried Eggs

4 hard-boiled eggs

3 tbsp mayonnaise

1 tsp curry powder

1 tbsp chutney (like Branston pickle)

1 tsp paprika

Method

1. Slice the eggs lengthwise and take out the yolks.
2. Mash the yolks with the chutney, curry powder and the mayonnaise.
3. Fill the egg whites with the mixture and arrange on a dish. Sprinkle with paprika and serve.

They are well worth a try if you like eggs, and also pretty good the next day chopped up as a sandwich filling!

Devils on Horseback

Another delicious treat – not seen very often today, but still really tasty. Personally, I don't think the fried bread really adds anything to the recipe.

Cooked prunes (or ready to eat prunes)

Streaky bacon

Grated cheddar cheese

Fried bread

Method

1. Remove the stone from the prune and stuff with grated cheese.
2. Roll streaky bacon round the prune and secure with a cocktail stick.
3. Put on a baking tray and cook for 10 minutes until the bacon is brown.
4. At the same time, spread fingers of bread with dripping or cooking fat and put on a tray in the oven.
5. Serve each prune on a finger of fried bread.

Danish Open Sandwiches

Open sandwiches were very popular at buffet meals in the 1970s. Each slice of bread should be buttered and covered with lettuce before putting on a selection of the following toppings:

Scrambled egg and smoked salmon

Rings of Danish salami topped with cottage cheese and sprinkled with chives

Cottage cheese and a slice of tinned peach

A slice of beef topped with horseradish sauce

A slice of pork with applesauce

Liver pate and sliced gherkins

Blue cheese topped with a little mayonnaise and onion rings

Cottage cheese, walnuts and apple slices

Scrambled egg and a crisscross of anchovy fillets

Tinned tuna mixed with
mayonnaise and sweet corn

Sliced ham topped with potato
salad and sprinkled with chives

Sliced hard-boiled egg with
a teaspoonful of Lumpfisk
caviar on top (available in most
supermarkets)

These sandwiches would also be decorated with garnishes of all kinds, and were the size of a quarter of a slice of bread, cut into either triangles or squares.

Main meals

Beef Bourguignon

175 g streaky bacon

40 g lard

1 kg steak, cut into cubes

2 tbsp flour

300 ml burgundy or full bodied
red wine

150 ml beef stock

450 g baby carrots, scraped and
left whole

Salt and pepper

12 small onions, blanched and
peeled whole

225 g button mushrooms

2 tbsp fresh parsley, finely
chopped

Method

1. Fry the bacon in the fat until nice and crispy.
2. Put the bacon in the casserole. Add the meat to the pan and brown on all sides.
3. Add the beef to the casserole dish and sprinkle the flour in the pan. Stir until it browns.
4. Put the stock and wine in the pan and bring to the boil. Then pour over the meat.
5. Add the rest of the ingredients apart from the onions and mushrooms and cover the casserole. Place in a preheated moderate oven for 1½ hours.
6. Add the onions and mushrooms and put back in the oven for another 30 minutes until the onions are tender.
7. Adjust the seasoning if necessary and put into a dish. Sprinkle with the parsley and serve with new potatoes.

Mixed Grill

A variety of the following meats:
Steak, lamb chops, kidney,
sausage, liver

225 g tomatoes halved

225 g mushrooms (button)

Watercress to garnish

Game chips (see below)

Method

1. Grill the meats that require the longest cooking time first, and then gradually add the other meats.
2. Grill the tomato halves and toss the mushrooms in a pan of melted butter, seasoned with salt and pepper.
3. For the game chips, peel potatoes and cut into thin slices (using a potato peeler). Soak in cold water, dry thoroughly and fry in deep fat until golden brown.
4. Serve the meat on an oblong plate with the mushrooms and tomatoes and garnish with watercress, placing the game chips to one side.

Trout Almandine

4 medium-sized trout

4 tbsp flour

½ tsp salt

100 g butter

2 tsp olive oil

75 g flaked almonds

100 g peeled prawns

1 tbsp parsley

Method

1. Wash the trout and dry with kitchen paper.
2. Mix the flour with the salt and dust over the fish.
3. Fry the fish in oil and 75 g of the butter in a pan until cooked and golden on both sides.
4. Add the remaining butter to the pan and on a low heat cook the almonds until they are golden.
5. Toss in the prawns and heat through.
6. Pour the prawn and almond butter onto the fish on a plate and sprinkle with parsley. Serve with sauté potatoes and peas.

Chicken Tikka Masala

This is a very British dish now. It is thought to have been invented in a Bangladeshi restaurant in Glasgow in the 1960s when a customer said that the chicken tikka was too dry, and asked to have some gravy with it. The chef is then said to have devised a sauce out of tomato soup, yoghurt and spices for him. Whether this account is true or not, we know that the dish was invented in order to adapt an Indian dish to suit the British palate.

Marinade

300 g skinned and boned chicken breast

3 tbsp yoghurt

1 tsp lemon juice

1 tsp turmeric

1 tsp coriander

2 tsp cumin

½ tsp ginger

1 garlic clove, crushed

1 tsp salt

Tikka masala paste

1 onion, chopped finely

1 piece fresh ginger

2 cloves garlic

3 tbsp olive oil

½ tsp chilli powder

4 tbsp tomato purée

1 tsp salt

4 tbsp double cream

1 bunch of fresh coriander

Method

1. Mix all the marinade ingredients together and coat the chicken. Leave in the fridge overnight.
2. In a pan, fry the onion in the oil over a slow heat until it is cooked and turning brown.
3. Add the ginger, garlic and spices and cook in the oil for 1 minute.
4. Stir in the tomato paste and stir continuously for 2 minutes.
5. Add the marinated chicken and cook for 15 minutes over a medium heat with the lid on.
6. Add the cream and stir for another 3 minutes.
7. Serve at once with white boiled rice and sprinkle with chopped fresh coriander leaves.

Desserts

Pear Conde

You never see this anymore, but it was everywhere in the 1960s, especially in canteen buffets as I remember. It really is very nice though, so try it!

4 cooking pears
600 ml milk
50 g pudding rice
1 tbsp sugar
2 tbsp water
1 tbsp powdered gelatine
4 tbsp red jam (no pips)

Method

1. Peel and cut the pears in half and core them. Stew in water until tender.
2. Cook the rice, milk and sugar in a double saucepan until creamy.
3. Soak the gelatine in 2 tsp of water and boil the jam in the remaining water. Then add to the soaked gelatine.
4. Place a spoonful of cold rice pudding in the bottom of a glass.
5. Arrange two pear halves on top.
6. When the jam mixture is cool and syrupy, pour gently over the pears and chill before serving.

Blackcurrant Pie

This is a pie you never see anymore, but it is really delicious. You will need to go to a fruit farm for the blackcurrants if you don't have your own bushes, because they don't sell them fresh in the shops any more,

225 g rich short crust pastry (see below)

1 kg blackcurrants

124 g sugar

Caster sugar to glaze

Method

1. Make the pastry and line a pie dish with it.
2. Pick over the fruit to check there are no bits of stem or mould and put half in the pie dish.
3. Sprinkle half the sugar over the currants. Then put the rest of the currants in and top with the remaining sugar.
4. Put a pastry lid on and brush with beaten egg white and caster sugar to glaze it.
5. Bake in a moderate oven for 40 minutes.

Baked Apple Dumplings

I made these in Domestic Science class and remember nibbling them on the way home as I carried them in a basket topped with a gingham tablecloth. There was not much left of one of them by the time I got home either! They are incredibly simple to make, but so delicious. Hanna Glasse in the eighteenth century had a recipe for apple dumplings, in which the pastry case for the apple was put into individual pudding cloths and boiled in water, rather than baking it. But I tend to think that baking is nicer.

4 large cooking apples

50 g butter

50 g brown sugar

50 g raisins or currants

½ tsp cinnamon

225 g rich short crust pastry (see p.122)

Method

1. Peel and core the apples.
2. Mix together the melted butter, sugar, raisins and cinnamon.
3. Stuff the mixture into the cavities of the apples.
4. Roll out the pastry into 4 big circles (use a dinner plate as a cutter).
5. Sit each apple in the middle of the pastry circle, pull it up and dampen the end to make a good seal.
6. Bake in a slow oven for 1½ hours. Enjoy!

Rich Short Crust Pastry

225 g flour

150 g fat (75 g butter and 50 g lard)

A pinch of salt

25 g caster sugar

1 egg

Method

1. Sieve flour and salt into a bowl and rub in the fat until it is like fine breadcrumbs.
2. Add sugar and bind together with enough egg to make a stiff paste.
3. Put in the fridge for 1 hour before use.

Upside Down Pineapple Cake

I remember seeing Fanny Cradock do this on a TV show in black and white, and it still looked good enough to eat! My mother used to make it for special family dinners.

Base

50 g butter

50 g caster sugar

1 tin pineapple rings

1 jar maraschino cherries

Cake

125 g butter

125 g sugar

150 g plain flour

1 rounded tsp baking powder

2 eggs

1 tsp vanilla essence

Method

1. Cream the butter and sugar together and spread it at the bottom of a round ovenproof dish.
2. Drain and dry the pineapple rings and arrange them on the dish. Make half moons around the edge and a circle in the middle, putting a cherry in the middle of each half moon and one in the centre.
3. Cream the butter and sugar and then beat in the eggs and vanilla essence.
4. Mix the baking powder and flour together and fold this into the egg mixture with a metal spoon.
5. Pour this mixture over the pineapples and cherries.
6. Bake in a moderate oven for 35–40 minutes until golden.
7. Turn out onto a plate to be seen in all its caramelised-base glory!

Please note that I am not including a Christmas section for the post war period because it would only contain more or less the same recipes that we use today.

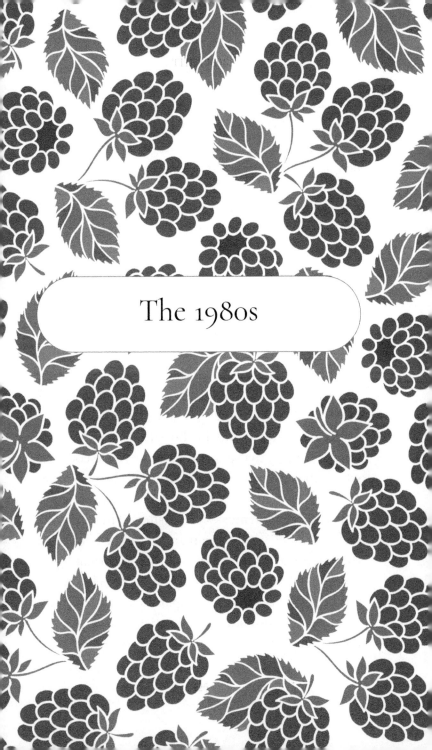

The 1980s

THE 1980s MEANT very different things to various branches of British society. Due to a global recession, unemployment peaked at more than 3 million people by 1984. Those in work were asked to accept a pay cut in order to keep themselves from being unemployed, so low-cost family meals were essential for a significant portion of the population.

Most homes had a microwave oven and a freezer, used to make not just 'quick' meals, but inexpensive ones, too. Before the 1980s, the majority of women were housewives and had time to prepare cheap cuts of meat to make meals for their families. Due to the recession most of those housewives had to get jobs and contribute to the family income. As a consequence, they didn't have a lot of time to spend in the kitchen when they got home from work.

Frozen food could be bought from the new freezer centres that popped up around the country, which took advantage of the situation by providing a wealth of ready meals packaged with tantalising pictures of gourmet-style dishes. These dishes seemed unbelievably cheap and could be cooked in the microwave from frozen in no more than eight minutes, all the while reducing the cost of electricity.

The majority of large companies at the time had staff canteens providing substantial, two-course hot meals that were subsidised for the workers. If both parents were working, they could get a cooked lunch and at the same time their children could get one at school. The family then only had to make a light supper for their evening meal.

Unfortunately, the pre-packed sandwich was introduced to staff canteens at this time. Sandwiches transformed lunchtime from an expensive and social activity (from the companies' point of view) to a solitary one, eaten at the desk or in the delivery van. The only alternative – if hot water was available – was a pot noodle. This was hot and filling, but more or less devoid of nutrition.

Another segment of British society lived a very different lifestyle during these years. This comprised the professional middle classes and so-called 'yuppies' (young, upwardly mobile professionals), who had benefited from the post-war boom and free university degrees. They qualified just in time to enter the blossoming financial, media and service industries in the city. The women had big hair and shoulder pads, and they all wore designer clothes and went on exotic holidays. They took over large parts of the post-industrial dockland areas of London and converted them into warehouse apartments, with views over the Thames.

They enjoyed the high-end culinary trend of nouvelle cuisine – tiny, artistically arranged pieces of food served in Michelin-star restaurants. This movement was in contrast to the butter-rich sauces of classic French cuisine. Another culinary trend of the 1980s was stacking food. Chefs would meticulously stack the food they were preparing into tall towers, which looked very impressive when served. The challenge for the customer was how to take the tower down without it looking like a mess on the plate, or worst of all falling onto the tablecloth.

Yuppies were said to eat out every night in London. The River Café, on the north bank of the Thames in Hammersmith, was established, serving what it termed inspirational, simple Italian cooking. The chefs would go to the produce market, just like an Italian housewife would do in Trentino. They would then write the menu for the day from the ingredients that inspired them. When the River Café first opened it only sold lunches to the surrounding businesses. Within a year it was so popular you couldn't get a table without booking well in advance.

In 1987, the extravagant lifestyle of the yuppies came to an end on 'Black Monday', when the stock market suddenly crashed. No longer could they eat out every night, but only once a month instead. The Italian food they had come to love had to be cooked at home. This was helped by the sudden import of Italian ingredients such as pasta, sun-dried tomatoes, pesto, olives, balsamic vinegar and extra-virgin olive oil. For the first time, supermarket shelves had entire sections devoted to Italian food, while the bread section sold fresh ciabatta. Garlic bread became the favourite starter for most people as they did not even have to make it themselves: it was readily available in the chilled cabinet of the supermarket. These Italian imports were in part responsible for a new food trend called the Slow Food movement, founded by Italian Carlo Petrini, which promoted a traditional and sustainable food ethic and emphasised the importance of local produce. It was a style of cooking that encompasses what we now call the healthy Mediterranean diet.

Vegetarian food became popular in the late 1980s, too, whereas in the previous decade it was thought to be hippy food. The benefits of meat-free meals once or twice a week were suggested by the medical profession. Linda McCartney wrote a vegetarian cookbook and launched a range of chilled and frozen healthy ready meals. These were very popular, mainly because they were still quick and convenient, but also because they were thought to be good for you.

One can't really look at 1980s food in Britain without looking at slimming diets. By 1984 the Ministry of Health had declared an obesity crisis in the UK. The unemployed, with their quick, microwaved ready meals, were eating volumes of cheap carbohydrates and not getting enough fresh food in their diets. Newspapers carried dire health warnings about diabetes epidemics. Wealthy yuppies and the professional middle classes had other concerns about their health. They were worried about heart attacks due to the stress of their jobs and their rich diets.

Every few weeks there was new medical advice on what sort of diet would not only slim you down but also prevent a heart attack or diabetes. The previously unheard of semi-skimmed milk was introduced into Britain to help with the problem of ill health, because animal fat was thought to be one of its main causes.

This gave food manufacturers an opportunity to stock our trolleys with processed low-fat foods to help the nation to get healthy, packed though they were with sugar, artificial sweeteners and filling carbohydrates. Fashionable diets of the time included the F-plan and Rosemary Conley's diet. These were high-fibre, low-fat diets with the addition of exercise. Suddenly diet gurus were everywhere; if you wanted to get ahead, you had to get a diet! There were meal supplements such as Slimfast shakes and chewy sweets called Ayds that were full of fibre, which you had to eat before each meal to fill you up.

The cabbage soup diet, then known as the Russian peasant diet, was very popular. The idea was that if you ate nothing but soup for a week you could rapidly lose a lot of weight. Unfortunately, lots of people went on the diet for much longer than a week and made themselves ill.

As you can see, everyday food in the 1980s is a very complex subject! In order to get a taste of the past from each group in society I have divided the recipes for this period. 'Quick, Budget Food' reflects the meals consumed by low-income households. Then comes the stark contrast of 'Yuppie Food', enjoyed by the wealthy when the economy was booming. This section reflects the international lifestyle of the yuppies and the sort of food that was eaten in fashionable restaurants. It is followed by a section on the increasingly popular 'Vegetarian Food' movement, as people became more aware of their health and animal welfare. Lastly, I have included 'Mediterranean Health Diet' recipes. This was the Slow Food diet that was recommended by health officials to stop the rising tide of obesity in the country. Medical researchers had realised that the low-fat, high-carbohydrate food that was thought to be good for everyone was in fact making the problem worse. The mixture of fresh vegetables, fish and fruit of the Mediterranean diet was thought to be much better for our bodies. In essence, it still is.

Quick, Budget Food

Ham Hock (Microwaved)

Ham hock is a very cheap cut of meat that can be served hot with parsley or mustard sauce, made into ham and mushroom pie or used in sandwiches. Even the stock it is cooked in can be made into pea and ham soup.

500 g smoked ham split in half

500 ml water

Method

1. Put the ham hock and water in a plastic or glass bowl and cover tightly with two sheets of microwave plastic wrap. Cook at 100 per cent for 35 minutes.
2. Remove from oven. Pierce plastic with the tip of a sharp knife and uncover, carefully avoiding the hot steam.

Cheddar Pudding

115 g breadcrumbs

300 ml milk

115 g cheddar cheese

1 egg, separated

1 tsp made English mustard

30 g butter melted

Salt and pepper

Method

1. Soak the breadcrumbs in the milk.
2. Mix in the grated cheese, the mustard and melted butter.
3. Stir in the egg yolk.
4. Whisk the egg white until stiff and fold gently into the cheese mixture.
5. Put into a buttered pie dish and bake in a moderate oven for 30 minutes until the top is brown.

Cheesy Rice

115 g rice

450 ml milk

150 ml water

30 g butter

115 g cheese

Salt and pepper

1 tsp mustard

Method

1. Wash the rice and boil in milk and water until soft and most of the liquid is absorbed.
2. Add the seasoning and mustard and mix well.
3. Butter a pie dish and put half the rice in it and top with half the grated cheese.
4. Put the remainder of the rice on top and then the rest of the cheese.
5. Dot with butter and brown in a hot oven and serve with green vegetables.

Chilli con Carne

100 g minced beef	
1 onion chopped	
1 clove of garlic	
½ tsp chilli powder	
227 g can of tomatoes	
1 tbs tomato purée	
213 g can kidney beans	

Method

1. Brown the beef in a pan.
2. Add the onions and garlic and cook until soft.
3. Add the tomatoes, chilli and purée cover and simmer for 20 minutes.
4. Add the drained kidney beans and cook for another 10 minutes.
5. Serve with boiled rice.

Spaghetti with Tuna

450 g spaghetti

Salt and pepper

185 g can of tuna

295 g can of condensed cream of celery soup

1 tbs chopped parsley

Rind of a small lemon

Grated Parmesan cheese

Method

1. Cook the spaghetti for 10 minutes in plenty of boiling, salted water and drain.
2. Mix the remaining ingredients in a bowl and add to the drained spaghetti in the saucepan.
3. Serve in a hot bowl and sprinkle with Parmesan cheese to taste.

Savoury Frankfurter Bake

2 medium potatoes peeled

1 onion chopped

100 g cheese

1 egg

200 g tin of sweet corn

1 jar frankfurter sausages

2 tomatoes sliced

Knob butter

Method

1. Boil the onion and potato together until soft and drain and mash and add a knob of butter.
2. Add half the cheese and a beaten egg and season.
3. Spread the potato on the base of an oven dish.
4. Place the frankfurters on top and then sprinkle with the sweet corn.
5. Cover with the rest of the cheese and arrange the sliced tomatoes on top.
6. Bake in a hot oven for about 20 minutes until the cheese is golden brown.

Tuna Pie

The next recipe uses condensed mushroom soup for the sauce and very strangely tastes like a chicken pie even though it is made with tuna!

250 g short crust pastry
185 g can of tuna in oil
1 can condensed cream of mushroom soup
1 small finely chopped onion
125 g chopped mushrooms
2 tbs grated Parmesan cheese
2 tsp lemon juice
1 tbs finely chopped fresh parsley
⅛ tsp celery seed
⅛ tsp thyme
120 ml milk

Method

1. Line a pie dish with half the pastry.
2. Drain the oil from the can of tuna and put 1 tbsp into a pan and sauté the onions until soft.
3. Add the mushrooms and cook for 5 minutes then add the mushroom soup stir and remove from the heat.
4. Add the cheese, lemon juice and herbs and the milk.
5. Lay the tuna on the pastry lined dish and cover with the other ingredients.
6. Top with the rest of the rolled pastry, crimp the edges of the pie and cut a few slits into the top to let the steam escape and brush with milk.
7. Bake in a medium hot oven for 35 minutes until the pastry is brown.

Dry Fried Curried Chicken with Spinach

Here is a recipe that really demonstrates instant cooking. It does not taste like a chicken curry we would recognise today, but if you are brave and adventurous have a go. I might be wrong, you might think it is delicious; it is certainly very quick!

450 g frozen leaf spinach

150 g frozen onion slices

1 tbs water

1 tsp garlic powder

1 tsp ground ginger

2 tsp curry powder

4 frozen chicken breasts (thawed and boned)

2 tsp gravy powder

4 tbs natural yoghurt

Method

1. Put the spinach, onion water and garlic and ginger in a bowl. Cover loosely and microwave on high for 5 minutes. Then stir and add the curry powder.
2. Microwave on high again for 4 minutes until the vegetables are soft, stir once and leave to stand.
3. Cut the thawed chicken into strips, put into a bag with the gravy powder, seal and toss the bag until the chicken is coated thoroughly. Put onto a microwave plate, loosely cover with greaseproof paper and cook on high for 30 seconds. Stir and cook again for 10 seconds. Add the chicken to the other ingredients and mix well. Cover and cook on high for 1 minute.
4. Check the seasoning and serve with a spoonful of yoghurt.

Baked Bean and Sausage Pie

You can't get simpler than this recipe, but I imagine it would still be a winner with most children after school.

1 pkt frozen ready rolled puff pastry (thawed)

2 cans baked beans and sausages

125 g grated cheddar cheese

Method

1. Line the base of a pie dish with the pastry.
2. Pour the two cans of baked beans and sausages onto the pastry.
3. Sprinkle with the grated cheese.
4. Top with the reminder of the pastry and brush with milk.
5. Bake in a medium oven for 30 minutes until the pastry is golden brown.
6. Serve with potatoes microwaved in their jackets.

Crispy Fish Pie

4 × 170g frozen cod in parsley
sauce, vacuum packed

1 can sweet corn

1 small pkt frozen prawns

4 pkt ready salted crisps

125 g grated cheddar cheese

1 bag frozen oven chips

Method

1. Simmer the bags of cod in parsley sauce in a pan of water for 15 minutes.
2. Take the cod and sauce out of the bags and put in a dish and flake the fish.
3. Add the drained sweet corn and frozen prawns.
4. Mix the crisps with the cheese and sprinkle on top.
5. Put a tray of oven chips in the oven with the fish pie and bake for 30 minutes. Serve at once.

Oven-Baked Spaghetti

This could not be simpler to make and would make a quick, tasty lunch.

225g wholewheat spaghetti (pre-cooked)

2 × 400g tins chopped tomatoes

1 large onion grated

1 tsp oregano

Salt and pepper

120 g cheddar cheese sliced

2 tbs Parmesan cheese

Method

1. Grease 4 ovenproof dishes and put a quarter of the spaghetti in each.
2. Mix the tinned tomatoes in a bowl with the grated onions, oregano and seasoning.
3. Evenly distribute the tomato mixture over the top of the spaghetti.
4. Place the cheese slices over the top of the spaghetti.
5. Sprinkle with the Parmesan and bake in a moderate oven for 25 minutes. Serve immediately with garlic bread.

Dessert

Banoffee Pie

Banoffee pie first came to supermarket shelves in 1984 but it was such a simple recipe it could be made using ingredients off the supermarket shelf.

1 sweet flan pastry case

3 bananas just ripe

1 jar caramel sauce

1 aerosol can of cream

Method

1. Cover the pastry case with the caramel sauce.
2. Slice the bananas and cover the caramel sauce with them.
3. Just before you are ready to serve, cover the bananas with circles of the aerosol cream and serve immediately otherwise the aerated cream deflates, making it not quite so impressive.

Caramel Custard

Sterilised, or long-life milk, as it is called today, gives this next recipe a really creamy taste while keeping it low cost. Apart from the eggs, everything can come from in the store cupboard.

2 large eggs
2 tsp dark brown sugar
Nutmeg to dust
240 ml sterilised milk

Method

1. Whisk the egg and sugar into the milk.
2. Pour the mixture into a small pudding dish and cover with foil.
3. Put the dish in a saucepan and pour enough boiling water to come to the base of the dish.
4. Simmer for 15 minutes and then leave in the pan to cool.
5. When cold turn the dish out onto a plate and sprinkle with nutmeg and serve immediately.

Apple and Blackberry Batter Pudding

450 g frozen sliced apple, thawed

225 g frozen blackberries

3 eggs

250 ml milk

1 tbs oil

3 tbs castor sugar

3 tbs plain flour

Method

1. Butter a shallow ovenproof dish and line the base with apples and top with the blackberries.
2. Put the flour and sugar in a bowl and mix; break in the eggs one at a time.
3. Gradually beat in the milk until you have a batter.
4. Add the oil and gently pour over the fruit.
5. Bake in a moderate oven for 25 minutes until set.
6. Serve immediately with cream or ice cream.

Quick, Budget Christmas Food

Boxing Day Cold Buffet: Chicken and Mushroom Vol-au-Vent

Vol-au-vents were the big thing for parties at Christmas, christenings and weddings in the 1980s. In the freezer section you could buy pre-cut vol-au vents, but I am giving you the **method** if you just want to buy rolled flaky or puff pastry and make the cases yourself.

Pastry

1. Roll out and with two cutters, one a centimetre larger than the other, cut out the larger rounds out and then cut halfway through each ring with the smaller cutter. Brush with egg wash.
2. Place on a baking tray and bake in a hot oven for 10 to 15 minutes.
3. Take from the oven and remove the centre cut, which will be the lid.

Filling

50 g butter

1 small onion finely chopped

100 g cooked chicken

1 x 290 g can condensed mushroom soup

1 tbs grated lemon rind

1 tbs finely chopped parsley

Salt and pepper to taste

Method

1. Fry onion in the butter until soft.
2. Mix in all the other ingredients
3. Spoon the mixture into the vol-au-vent cases and top with pastry lid.
4. Bake in a moderate oven for 10 minutes and serve immediately.

This is a perfect salad dish that will last a week in a fridge. It can be added to any cold buffet along with a simple potato salad and a green salad, or just eaten for supper with cold turkey or ham.

Curried Pasta Salad

225 g pasta (any shape)

1 large onion finely chopped

1 tbs oil

150 ml mayonnaise

1 tbs mild curry paste (such as korma)

2 tbs mango chutney

Method

1. Cook the pasta and drain.
2. Fry the onion in the oil until transparent.
3. Mix the curry paste with the onions and cook for 1 minute.
4. Leave until cold and then add the mango chutney and mayonnaise and cold, drained pasta.

I can guarantee that once made, this dish will be a family favourite!

Cold Garlic Turkey

This recipe can be made from leftover turkey breast and will be a talking point at any Christmas buffet with the curried pasta salad. I have been making both recipes every year at Christmas since the 1980s and my family would certainly complain if they were not both on the Boxing Day buffet table.

250 g cold cooked turkey breast meat chopped

125 g chopped dill pickle

50 g chopped capers

125 g chopped green olives

150 ml mayonnaise

1 garlic clove crushed

Method

1. Mix all the chopped ingredients together.
2. Serve in a bowl with a sprig of parsley.

Honey-Glazed Sausages

Nothing is more delicious or inexpensive to make than honey-glazed sausages at a buffet, either hot or cold.

24 sausages

5 tbs clear honey

4 tsp soy sauce

Finely grated rind of 1 lemon

3 tbs cider vinegar

4 tsp whole grain mustard

Method

1. Make the glaze by mixing all the ingredients apart from the sausages together.
2. Put the sausages in a roasting tin and prick all over with a fork.
3. Pour over the marinade evenly and cover and leave for 1 hour.
4. Turn the sausages in the marinade and put them in a hot oven for 15 minutes, taking out and turning every so often so they are fully coated in the sauce.
5. Check the sausages are fully cooked by cutting one in half and serve immediately, or leave until cold before serving.

Salmon Horseshoe Ring

This recipe is made with scone mix instead of pastry and shaped like a horseshoe on the baking tray before baking. It is easy to make and actually very tasty and impressive-looking for a Christmas dinner party for very little cost.

Scone mix

225 g plain flour
1 tsp salt
2 tsp baking powder
55 g hard margarine
Milk to mix to a stiff dough

Filling

30 g butter
1 heaped tbsp cornflour
150 ml milk
185 g can salmon
1 tsp chopped capers
1 tsp lemon juice
1 tbs chopped fresh parsley
Egg or milk for glaze

Method

1. Make a sauce by melting the butter in a pan, then adding the cornflour and milk mixed together with the seasoning. Stir on a low heat until thickened, then take off the heat and add the salmon, capers and lemon juice and mix well.
2. Make the scone mix by rubbing in the margarine to the flour and other ingredients and bind with milk. Roll out on a floured board in a thin rectangular shape.
3. Spread the cold filling along the long side of the rectangle and roll it up like a sausage roll. Moisten the edges with water to make it stick.
4. Carefully move it onto a baking tray and pull the ends together to make a horseshoe shape.
5. With a pair of kitchen scissors or a knife, make some cuts about two-thirds of the way into the filled roll. Turn each section on its side so that the filling is exposed a little.
6. Glaze with egg or milk and bake for 15 to 20 minutes in a hot oven. Serve when warm with a salad or hot with vegetables for a main meal.

Dessert

Baked Alaska

This is incredibly simple to make, but very impressive for a quick Christmas dinner party dessert.

22 cm bought sponge flan case

485 g block of vanilla ice cream

382 g can blackberries drained

3 egg whites

150 g castor sugar

Method

1. Put the sponge base on a heat-proof plate.
2. Place the block of ice cream in the sponge base and smooth to a dome-shaped top.
3. Spoon the blackberries over the ice cream.
4. Whisk the egg whites until stiff, beating the sugar in a little at a time.
5. Cover the ice cream and sponge base with the meringue and bake in a hot oven for 5 minutes.
6. Serve immediately.

Budget Christmas Cake (Microwaved)

During the 1980s there were 'Scoop and Save' shops all over Britain where you bagged and measured a large variety of foods for yourself from big drums for very low cost. You could get just the ingredients for a cake like this without having to buy a bag of every different fruit. You could buy all your dry ingredients in this way, even, believe it or not, dried egg powder! At this time you could also go to off-licences and buy sherry on tap, providing you were over 18 and took your own bottles.

175 g sultanas

175 g raisins

100 g currants

75 g glacé cherries

75 g mixed peel

150 ml sherry

175 g margarine

175 g dark brown sugar

3 eggs (or dried equivalent)

100 g white plain flour

100 g white self-raising flour

½ tsp mixed spice

25 g ground almonds

Pinch of salt

250 g packet of marzipan

500 g icing sugar

Cake frill and cake decoration for show

Method

1. Put all the fruit including the cherries in a bowl and pour the sherry over them. Cover with cling film, pricking the top in two places, and microwave on full power for 3 minutes.
2. Leave the mixture to absorb the sherry overnight.
3. The next day, cream the margarine and sugar until light and fluffy, then gradually add the eggs one at a time, beating thoroughly.
4. Fold in the ground almonds, flours, spices and salt.
5. Stir in the fruit soaked in sherry.

6. Line a deep 20cm cake dish (not metal) with greaseproof paper and pour the mixture into it. Cook on low for 18 to 20 minutes.

7. Test the cake with a skewer and if it comes out clean it is cooked.

8. When cold, roll the marzipan out into a circle and top the cake with it.

9. Mix the icing sugar with enough water to make it spreadable and coat the top of the marzipan with it, whisking it up with a fork to look like snow. Add the decorations of your choice or a sprig of holly dusted with icing sugar.

10. Put a Christmas cake frill around the side and you have a quick and very reasonable Christmas cake for the family.

'Yuppie' Food

I have put more starter and canapé recipes than main meals in this section, as 'yuppies' were well known to eat out every night and were more likely to have people to their apartments for drinks and nibbles than a three-course meal.

Cocktail Party Food

Avocado Dip

1 large ripe avocado

1 tsp lemon juice

1 tsp Worcester sauce

75 g cream cheese

Salt and pepper

Method

1. Peel the avocado and mash the contents with a fork until smooth.
2. Add the lemon juice and Worcester sauce.
3. Beat the cream cheese until soft and mix with avocado and season to taste. Serve with celery sticks or bread sticks.

Anchovy Toast

Yuppies would have been used to this relish when they had more money to spare. It is called Patum Peperium or Gentleman's Relish, and you can still buy it in high-end delicatessens. This home-made version is just as nice.

3 tbsp olive oil

1 tbsp wine vinegar

2 tsp lemon juice

2 garlic cloves

Black pepper

Toasted sliced bread

2 × 50g tins of anchovies

Method

1. Put the anchovies in a blender with the oil from the can and the garlic and purée.
2. Slowly add the vinegar and then the oil drop by drop, as you would when making mayonnaise.
3. Season to taste with pepper and lemon juice.
4. Toast the bread and spread the paste on top then put under a hot grill for no more than 30 seconds.
5. Serve hot cut into squares or triangles.

Marmite Wheels

1 pkt frozen ready-rolled puff
pastry

1 tbsp Marmite

1 tsp water

Method

1. Place the rolled pastry on a floured board.
2. Mix the Marmite with the water.
3. Brush the Marmite mixture over the pastry, right to the edges.
4. Roll up the pastry like a Swiss roll.
5. Chill in the fridge for 1 hour.
6. With a sharp knife, cut very thin rings along the roll and put them on a baking tray.
7. Bake in a preheated, moderately hot oven for 10 minutes.
8. Serve hot, warm or cold.

Bacon and Olive Rolls

Jar of large pimento stuffed green olives
250 g finely grated cheddar cheese
1 pkt streaky bacon, de-rinded
1 pkt cocktail sticks

Method

1. Cut the olives in half lengthways and remove the pimento.
2. Chop the pimento and mix with the cheese. Return to the two halves of the olive, pressing them together so each olive is filled with cheese and pimento mixture.
3. Cut each bacon rasher into three and smooth them on a board with the back of a knife to make them thin.
4. Roll each piece of bacon around the olives and skewer in place with a cocktail stick.
5. Grill on a tray for five minutes until the bacon is cooked and crisp.
6. Serve at once. I guarantee they won't last long as this very simple canapé is really delicious.

Garlic Sausage Tubes

100 g garlic cream cheese (such as Boursin)

80 g cream cheese

250 g sliced French garlic sausage

1 pkt cocktail sticks

Method

1. Mix the garlic cheese and cream cheese thoroughly in a bowl and season if needed.
2. Divide the cheese between the slices of garlic sausage, spreading evenly over each slice.
3. Roll up the slices of sausage into tubes. Put three cocktail sticks into the tube, evenly spaced.
4. Cut into three and serve.

Buffalo Mozzarella and Tomato Canapés

1 pkt small buffalo mozzarella
balls

1 bunch fresh basil

1 pkt cherry tomatoes

1 pkt of cocktail sticks

Salt and pepper

Method

1. Drain the mozzarella balls and cut in half.
2. Cut the cherry tomatoes in half.
3. Skewer the tomato halves from the uncut side and slide in a couple of basil leaves onto the stick, and then the cut side of the mozzarella balls.
4. Serve with a sprinkle of salt and freshly ground pink pepper (very trendy at the time).

Danish Salami Horns

60 g cream cheese

4 sun-dried tomatoes, finely chopped

12 slices Danish salami

12 stoned black olives

Method

1. Mix the chopped tomatoes with the cream cheese and put in a piping bag with a large nozzle.
2. Coil the salami slices into cone shapes.
3. Pipe some of the cream cheese into the open end of the cone and place an olive in the middle.
4. With the cocktail stick, fold the end of the cone and weave the stick along it to secure it and make the cone easy to pick up with your hand.

Garlic Bread

Until the mid-1980s it was considered unsociable to eat garlic, as it makes your breath smell! But once garlic bread was tried, people realised that if everyone ate it then this was not a problem. It became the essential starter for every dinner party. This is a recipe that makes soft, juicy garlic bread or a crispy variety from the same ingredients.

1 French stick
100 g soft butter
2 small or 1 large garlic clove
2 tbsp of finely chopped fresh parsley
½ tsp celery seed (optional)

Method

1. Cut the French stick into neat, round, thin slices.
2. Mix the butter with the crushed garlic and herbs.
3. Line a baking tray with foil.
4. Spread the garlic butter on one side of the bread and arrange on an oven tray.
5. If you want soft garlic bread, cover with a sheet of foil; if you want them crispy, leave them uncovered.
6. Bake in a hot oven for 5 minutes.

Main Meals

Lamb in Mint Sauce

The use of cream and redcurrant sauce makes this dish particularly delicious. And yet it is very simple to create.

4 lamb chops
30 g butter
2 onions sliced in rings
2 tbsp flour
300 ml stock
4 tsp redcurrant Jelly
2 tsp mint sauce
2 tbsp single cream
Salt and pepper
Fresh mint to garnish

Method

1. Sprinkle the chops with seasoning on both sides.
2. Melt half the butter in a pan. Add the chops and cook for 10 minutes on each side. Transfer to a warm dish and keep hot.
3. Fry the onion in the rest of the butter in the pan until soft.
4. Stir in the flour and cook for 1 minute. Gradually blend in the stock, stirring until it thickens.
5. Add the redcurrant jelly and mint sauce, cream and season to taste.
6. Pour sauce over the chops and serve with boiled potatoes and peas.

Chicken Kiev

4 tbsp butter softened

1 garlic clove

1 tbsp finely chopped parsley

Salt and pepper

4 skinless, boned chicken breasts

85 g fresh breadcrumbs

2 beaten eggs

3 tbsp Parmesan cheese

Oil for frying

Method

1. Crush the garlic clove and put it in a bowl with the butter, parsley and seasoning, then mix well. Divide into four balls and put into the fridge to chill.
2. Flatten the chicken breasts until they are even thicknesses and then put the chilled balls of garlic butter in the middle. Fold the chicken over the butter and secure with a cocktail stick.
3. Mix the breadcrumbs with the Parmesan cheese.
4. Dip the chicken parcels in the beaten egg and then coat with the breadcrumb mixture. Put on a plate and chill for 1 hour in the fridge.
5. Gently remove the cocktail sticks and coat in the egg and breadcrumb mixture for a second time.
6. Put the oil in a deep-fat fryer and heat until a cube of bread put in browns in 30 seconds. Gently put in the Kievs one at a time for 5 minutes until they are cooked through. You could pan fry the Kievs on both sides if preferred and then finish the cooking by putting them in the oven for 10 minutes.

Lamb Pilaf

40 g butter

1 large onion peeled and chopped

500 g lean, boneless lamb cut into pieces

50 g pine nuts

25 g sultanas

Salt and pepper

1 tsp cinnamon

3 tbsp chopped parsley

3 tbsp tomato purée

500 g long-grain rice

1 litre water

Method

1. Cook the onion in the butter in a large heavy-based saucepan until soft.
2. Add the lamb and cook until browned all over.
3. Add the pine nuts until they brown.
4. Stir in the sultanas, salt, pepper, cinnamon, parley and tomato purée, then cover with water and stir well.
5. Bring to the boil and then simmer for 30 minutes, or until the meat is tender.
6. Add the rice and cover with water again.
7. Simmer gently, covered and undisturbed, for 20 minutes until the rice is cooked and has absorbed the water.
8. Serve immediately.

Chinese Sticky Ribs

1 kg pork rib

4 tbsp dark soy sauce

3 tbsp muscovado sugar

1 tbsp oil

2 garlic cloves

3 tsp five-spice powder

1 piece root ginger, grated

Shredded spring onions

Method

1. Put the ribs in a shallow dish.
2. Mix all the other ingredients in a bowl apart from the spring onions.
3. Rub the mixture well into the ribs, then cover the dish with cling film and chill for 6 hours in the fridge.
4. Either cook them on a barbecue or in an oven on a rack over a tray for 30 to 40 minutes, basting with the marinade whenever the ribs look dry.
5. Serve with shredded spring onions on top.

Desserts

Kiwi Fruit Pavlovas

1 pkt meringue nests

150 ml extra thick double cream

I pkt kiwi fruit

A few mint sprigs for garnishing

Method

1. Put each meringue nest on an individual plate.
2. Gently, so as not to break the meringue, spoon the double cream into the middle.
3. Arrange slices of peeled kiwi fruit on top.
4. Add a small sprig of mint to garnish and serve.

Baked Stem Ginger Cheesecake with Sour Cream Topping

If you like cheesecake and ginger, I highly recommend this recipe. It would grace any high-end restaurant in 1980s London or today.

150 ml soured or cultured cream

125 g ginger biscuits

50 g butter, melted

2 tbsp syrup from stem ginger jar

4 pieces stem ginger, chopped

225 g cottage cheese

225 g cream cheese

2 eggs

200 g castor sugar

Pinch of salt

Method

1. Grease a loose-bottomed cake tin.
2. Put the biscuits in a bag and break them into crumbs with a rolling pin. Combine the biscuit crumbs with the melted butter and press into the cake tin.
3. Press the cottage cheese through a sieve with the back of a spoon and mix it with the cream cheese, ginger syrup, chopped stem ginger and salt.
4. Whisk the eggs with 150g of the castor sugar until thick and light in colour.
5. Gradually mix in the cheese mixture and pour onto the biscuit base.
6. Bake in a preheated moderate oven for 30 to 40 minutes until set and firm to touch. Turn off the oven, open the door and leave the cheesecake to go cold in the oven.
7. Mix the remaining 50g castor sugar with the soured cream and pour over the cheesecake, then chill in the fridge overnight.
8. Remove from the tin and serve.

'Yuppie' Christmas Food

Christmas Breakfast

Hot Cherry Croissant with Kirsch

4 croissants
1 jar cherries in syrup
1 tbsp kirsch
1 tbsp cornflour
Double cream to serve

Method

1. Drain the cherries and keep the juice.
2. Add the 1 tbsp cornflour to the liquid and put in a pan to thicken. Add the cherries to the sauce with the kirsch and set aside until cold.
3. Fill the croissants with the cherry compote and put them on a tray in the oven. Cook for 5 minutes to crisp the croissant and warm the filling.
4. Serve at once with cream.

Starter

Minted Orange and Melon

This is a simple, but light and refreshing starter that is perfect to eat before any rich Christmas food.

1 small honeydew melon

2 large sweet oranges

1 tbsp finely chopped fresh mint

Sprigs of mint to garnish

Method

1. Cut the melon into small pieces and put in a bowl.
2. Grate the rind off the oranges and sprinkle it onto the melon.
3. Segment the orange with a knife, cutting off all the membrane, and cut into bite-sized pieces.
4. Add the orange to the melon with the chopped mint and mix gently.
5. Put into individual dishes or glasses and chill, adding a sprig of mint just before serving.

Fish Course

Smoked Mackerel and Horseradish Sauce

4 smoked mackerel fillets

150 ml double cream

3 tsp ready made creamed horseradish sauce

Rind and juice of half a lemon

1¼ tsp salt

Watercress

Thinly sliced brown bread and butter to serve.

Method

1. Mix the horseradish sauce with the lemon rind, juice and cream.
2. Remove the skin from the mackerel and place fish on a platter or individual plates.
3. Spoon the sauce over the fish and garnish with watercress.
4. Serve with the bread and butter.

Main

Marbella Chicken

Yuppies most often ate out in restaurants, but when they did dine in they might well have made Marbella chicken. This could possibly have been the main course at Christmas in a 'yuppie' warehouse apartment. A dish like this in various forms was an outstanding favourite in restaurants at the time. This is my own version of the dish. It is perfect if you have a lot of guests to feed and don't want to spend all your time in the kitchen. The beauty of the dish is that the chicken is marinated the night before to absorb all the Spanish/ Moorish flavours. If you try this recipe you will see why even the cooking-shy Yuppies would have made it, because it requires very little effort and yet is an impressive dish to serve.

2 × 1½ kg whole chicken

200 g pitted prunes

100 g pimento-filled green olives

50 g caper berries (or capers if you
can't get them)

6 garlic cloves, crushed

50 ml balsamic vinegar

150 ml good red wine

1 tbsp brown sugar

2 bay leaves

4 tbsp olive oil

2 tsp salt

4 tbsp chopped fresh oregano

3 tbsp chopped parsley to decorate

Method

1. Dissect each of the chickens into four.
2. Place in a deep roasting tin large enough for them to be spaced apart.
3. Mix all the other ingredients together in a bowl, apart from the parsley.
4. Pour the marinade over the chickens, making sure they are all well coated.
5. Cover and leave in the fridge overnight.
6. The next day, about 1½ hours before serving, turn the chicken joints on the baking tray and sprinkle with the brown sugar.
7. Pour the wine around the outside of the chicken and spoon the other ingredients in between the chicken joints over the wine.
8. Put in a moderate oven and bake for 1 hour, basting with the marinade every so often while cooking. When the juices in the chicken run clean it is cooked.
9. Transfer the chicken joints into a large serving dish and spoon over the sauce. Sprinkle with parsley and serve with a variety of vegetables.

Dessert

Pineapple Sorbet

A pineapple filled with home-made pineapple sorbet would have been a very exotic and festive dessert at the time, yet it is very simple to make.

1 fresh, ripe pineapple

4 tbsp water

100 g icing sugar

Mint sprigs to decorate

Method

1. Cut the pineapple lengthwise in half and cut out the flesh with a knife, being careful not to cut through the shell of the fruit.
2. Discard the central hard core of the fruit and put the rest into a food processor with the water until puréed.
3. Add the icing sugar and pile the mixture into the two halves of the fruit shell. Cover and freeze until firm.
4. Take out of the freezer and put into the fridge 20 minutes before serving. Decorate with sprigs of mint.
5. Serve on a large platter and let your dinner guests help themselves with serving spoons.

Chestnut Charlotte

I am sure this would have been a favourite on the dessert trolley in a fashionable French restaurant in London at the time. It is not that difficult to make and very impressive for a festive dessert, but it is very rich so only give small portions or you will find a lot left on your guests' plates.

100 g unsalted butter

440 g can of unsweetened chestnut purée

225 g sugar

20 sponge fingers (as on p.232)

3 tbsp rum

5 tbsp water

Decoration

300 ml double cream

1 tbsp rum

1 chocolate flake

Method

1. Beat the butter and chestnut purée with a mixer until light and fluffy.
2. Put 175 g of the sugar and 4 tbs water in a pan and simmer until the sugar dissolves, stirring constantly. Then boil until the syrup thickens, stirring all the time.
3. Slowly beat the syrup into the chestnut mixture, then add the rum.
4. Put the remaining sugar and water into the pan and once dissolved bring to the boil until a golden brown colour.
5. Prepare a tall dish or cake tin and dip the length side of the sponge finger in the caramel, then put another biscuit next to it so the caramel sticks them together. Continue doing this until the all the sides of the tin are covered.
6. Cover the base of the mound with biscuits, gluing them together with the caramel.
7. Carefully spoon the chestnut mixture in the tin over the biscuit base.
8. Cover and put in the fridge overnight.
9. Turn the mound out and pipe around the top with whipped cream, then sprinkle with chocolate flakes.
10. The nice thing about this fabulous dessert is that it can be made the day before the festive dinner party, and I am sure it would impress any guest.

Vegetarian Food

Here are some of my family's favourite vegetarian recipes from the 1980s.

Cheesy Vegetable Chowder

This is a perfect dish to come back to on
a cold day after a morning walk.

225 g of potatoes peeled and cut
into small cubes

100 g grated carrot

100 g finely chopped celery

100 g cubed cucumber

30 g butter

500 ml milk

250 g grated cheddar

Salt and pepper to taste

Water

Method

1. Sauté the cucumber and celery in the butter until soft.
2. Add the carrot and potato and cover with water.
3. Cook until soft, then add the milk, cheese and seasoning and serve with lots of bread to dip into the soup.

Dhal

400 g red lentils

1 litre water

2 small bay leaves

2 garlic cloves

2 large onions, chopped

½ tsp ground ginger

½ tsp turmeric

2 tbsp oil

2 tsp garam masala

Salt and pepper

Method

1. Cover the lentils in boiling water and leave for 1 hour to soak.
2. Add the bay leaves, half the onions, half the garlic, the ginger and turmeric and simmer in a pan until soft.
3. While the lentils are cooking, sauté the rest of the onions and garlic in the oil until soft and just turning brown.
4. Add the garam masala and cook for 1 minute.
5. Stir this into the cooked lentils, stir and leave for 1 hour (you can leave it overnight for better flavour).
6. Reheat and serve piping hot with naan bread.

Curried Nut Roast

3 tbsp oil

1 onion, chopped

1 green pepper

175 g chopped tomatoes

175 g chopped hazelnuts or Brazil nuts

75 g brown breadcrumbs

1 clove of garlic

1 tsp mixed herbs

1 tsp dried parsley

1 tsp curry powder

1 egg

Salt and pepper

Method

1. Cook the onion and pepper in the oil until soft, then add the tomatoes.
2. Mix the nuts, breadcrumbs, garlic, herbs and curry powder in a bowl.
3. Stir in the cooked onion, pepper, tomatoes and the egg and mix well.
4. Put into a greased loaf tin and bake for 30 minutes until brown.
5. Serve either hot or cold with vegetables or a salad.

Mushroom Quiche

This is a tasty quiche to eat hot or cold. Interestingly, it is made with evaporated milk, which is still available in the supermarkets, even though it is not used as much as it was in the 1980s.

Pastry

225 g plain flour

⅛ tsp salt

115 g butter

1 egg

3 tbsp cold water

Filling

1 can button mushrooms (or just use a punnet of fresh)

2 eggs

½ can evaporated milk

55 g grated cheese

55 g butter

2 onions, chopped

¼ tsp English mustard

Method

1. Put all the pastry ingredients apart from the water into a food processor and mix well.
2. Add the cold water until it combines the mixture and chill in the fridge for 1 hour before using.
3. Line a dish with the chilled rolled-out pastry.
4. Cook the onion in the butter until soft. (If using fresh mushrooms add these to the pan and cook through.)
5. Beat the eggs and add the evaporated milk, grated cheese, seasoning and mustard. Mix until smooth.
6. Spread the sautéed mushrooms and onion onto the pastry base and pour over the egg mixture.
7. Bake in a moderate oven for 35 minutes, or until set to the touch and golden. Serve either hot with vegetables or cold with a salad for lunch.

Mushroom Cheesy Rice

800 g cooked rice

75 g mushrooms, chopped

2 garlic cloves

1 large onion, chopped

6 tbsp oil

1 tsp salt

½ tsp pepper

125 g grated cheese

1 tbsp parsley, finely chopped

Method

1. Cook the onions in the oil in a large frying pan or wok until soft, then add the mushrooms and garlic.
2. When the mushrooms are cooked, add the cooked rice, salt, pepper and grated cheese.
3. Cook for 5 minutes more, stirring constantly. Serve sprinkled with chopped parsley.

Nut and Vegetable Roast

6 carrots, grated

3 courgettes, sliced

1 celery stick, chopped

3 large onions, chopped

100 g mushrooms, sliced

300 g wholemeal flour

1 can drained butter beans

100 g of ground nuts (hazelnuts, walnuts or Brazil nuts ground in a hand grater like a Mouli grater, which was very popular at the time for grinding nuts and cheese)

4 tbs oil

70 g cheddar cheese, grated

1 tbsp soy sauce

1 tsp dried thyme

Salt and pepper

1 egg

Method

1. Sauté the vegetables in the oil in a wok or large saucepan until soft. Transfer to a large mixing bowl.
2. Add all the other ingredients apart from the egg and mix well until it forms a dough.
3. Put into an oiled loaf tin and brush with the beaten egg.
4. Bake for 45 minutes in a moderately hot oven until a knife inserted comes out clean.
5. Turn out onto a plate and serve hot with onion gravy or cold with a salad.

Onion Gravy

1 onion, finely chopped
20 g butter
20 g flour
300 ml vegetable stock
Salt and pepper
1 tsp soy sauce

Method

1. Fry the onion in the butter until light brown.
2. Add flour and cook for 1 minute.
3. Stir in the stock and soy sauce slowly.
4. Bring to the boil and simmer for 5 minutes.
5. Season and serve.

Dessert

Oat Fruit Crumble

400 g fruit (either apples, gooseberries or pears)

3 tbsp honey

2 tsp cinnamon

90 g wholewheat flour

150 g rolled oats

175 g soft butter

Method

1. Mix the flour, oats and cinnamon in a large bowl.
2. Add the butter in small pieces and mix well.
3. Place half the mixture in a greased, ovenproof dish and press down.
4. Layer the fruit on top and dot with honey.
5. Put the remaining crumble on top and bake in a pre-heated, moderate oven for 40 minutes.
6. Serve hot or cold with cream.

Black Carob Cake

180 g wholewheat flour

55 g carob flour

250 g butter

1.225 kg chopped mixed nuts

1 tsp vanilla extract

4 tbsp honey

5 whole almonds (for decoration)

Method

1. Cream the butter, honey and vanilla together.
2. Mix the flours in a separate bowl.
3. Mix into the butter and honey, add the nuts and beat well.
4. Put the mixture into a greased baking tray and decorate the top with the whole almonds.
5. Bake for 30 minutes in a moderate oven.
6. Serve hot or cold with cream.

Vegetarian Christmas Food

Alfalfa Sprouts and Scrambled Egg Toast

This was a favourite starter or sometimes a lunch dish with my vegetarian friends. We used to sprout all our own seeds at the time, but you can buy alfalfa sprouts in a good vegetarian food shop today.

I pkt alfalfa sprouts

4 large free-range eggs

50 ml single cream

25 g butter

Marmite

Salt and pepper

Wholemeal toast and butter

Method

1. Break the eggs into a bowl and add the cream and salt and pepper. Whisk.
2. Put the butter in a pan. Add the eggs and stir constantly until just scrambled.
3. Toast the bread while you are scrambling the eggs and spread with butter and marmite.
4. Top the toast with the scrambled eggs and then pile the alfalfa sprouts on top.
5. Cut into four and serve on individual plates as a wholesome starter.

Mushroom Nut Delight

When I was a vegetarian in the 1980s this was a favourite dinner party and Christmas dish. In autumn we used to pick field mushrooms, which intensified the flavour in the sauce.

Nut base

250 g soft brown breadcrumbs

125 g ground almonds

75 g finely chopped Brazil nuts

75 g pine nuts

60 g butter

1 garlic clove

½ tsp mixed herbs

Topping

500 g mushrooms (any kind you like)

60 g butter

2 heaped tbsp flour

425 ml milk

Salt and pepper, to taste

4 tomatoes

1 tbsp chopped fresh parsley

Method

1. First make the nut base. Mix the nuts and all the other ingredients together in a bowl, then rub in the butter.
2. Press into a heatproof dish and bake in a medium-hot oven for about 20 minutes until it browns.
3. Make the topping by slicing the mushrooms and sautéing them in the butter until soft. Add the flour and stir for a minute, then add the milk and keep stirring on a low heat until the sauce thickens. Pour this over the nut base.
4. Top with slices of tomato and return to the oven for about 20 minutes.
5. Sprinkle with parsley and serve with boiled new potatoes.

Walnut and Stilton Flan

Pastry

225 g plain flour

100 g butter

25 g walnuts

Pinch celery salt

Cold water

Filling

1 small leek

2 celery sticks

200 g Stilton cheese

200 ml double cream

25 g butter

3 egg yolks

Salt and pepper

Method

1. Butter a quiche dish.
2. Mix the flour, celery salt and walnuts in a food processor until they become a fine mixture.
3. Add the butter and process, then add enough water to combine the pastry dough.

4. Roll out the dough and line the quiche dish with it. Chill for 1 hour.
5. Put a circle of greaseproof paper on top of the pastry and top with dried beans. Bake for 10 minutes in a hot oven.
6. Remove the beans and greaseproof paper and set to one side while you make the filling.
7. Melt the butter in a pan and add the chopped celery and leek. Cook gently for 15 minutes.
8. Put the leeks and celery in a bowl and add the crumbled Stilton and 2 tbsp of the cream. Mix gently so as not to break up the Stilton pieces too much and season with salt and pepper.
9. Put the remaining cream in a pan and bring to a simmer. Pour over the egg yolks, stirring constantly.
10. Add this to the bowl of Stilton and vegetables and mix together, then spoon onto the pre-baked flan case.
11. Bake for 15 minutes until set and serve.

Dessert

Vegetarian Mincemeat

In the 1980s it was difficult to get vegetarian mincemeat in the shops because it was mostly produced with beef suet. This is an easy recipe and a lovely thing to give to vegetarian friends at Christmas.

500 g grated cooking apple

500 g raisins

250 g currants

300 g sultanas

75 g mixed peel

250 g grated cold butter

300 g soft brown sugar

Rind and juice of lemon and

1 orange

2 tsp mixed spice

4 tbsp brandy

Method

1. Mix all the ingredients together in a large bowl.
2. Put in sterilised jars and keep for 4 weeks before using.

Festive Carrot Cake

Cake

100 ml sunflower oil

2 eggs

Pinch of salt

130 g light brown sugar

125 g self-raising flour

1 tsp mixed spice

130 g grated carrots

25 g chopped walnuts

30 g whole glacé cherries

Topping

50 g soft butter

50 g cream cheese

225 g icing sugar

1 tsp sherry

Cherries, Angelica strips and
walnuts to decorate

Method

1. Lightly grease and line an 8in square cake tin. Preheat the oven.
2. Mix the flour, mixed spice and salt in a bowl and stir in the sugar.
3. Add the eggs and oil and mix well.
4. Put in the grated carrots, cherries and chopped walnuts.
5. Pour the mixture into the cake tin and bake in a moderate oven for 25 minutes or until firm to the touch. Leave to cool in the tin.
6. For the topping, beat the soft butter and cheese together. Add the icing sugar and the sherry and mix until it is light and fluffy.
7. When the cake is cold, turn it out of the tin and spread the icing over it and decorate with the cherries, Angelica strips and walnuts.

Almond Festive Crunch Pie

375 g pkt all-butter puff pastry

100 g ground almonds

1 tsp almond essence

2 eggs, separated

100 g butter

100 g light brown sugar

4 tbsp single cream

4 level tsp flour

Icing sugar

Method

1. Divide the pastry into half and roll them out into two rounds approx. 25cm diameter.
2. Cream the sugar and butter together, then beat in the yolk of the egg.
3. Add the ground almonds, almond essence, cream and mix well.
4. Spread the mixture onto one of the pastry rounds on a baking tin, leaving a gap at the edge to add the top layer.
5. Brush the edge with water and add the top round of pastry. Press firmly on the edge with a fork to seal them together.
6. Brush the top with the egg white and make long slits in the top to release the steam when cooking.
7. Bake for 20 minutes until it rises well and is brown, then sprinkle generously with icing sugar.
8. Serve this delicious festive pie when it is warm with lots of cream.

Mediterranean Healthy-Eating Food

Starters

Tomato Bruschetta

The main rule when making this delicious starter is to use a really ripe and flavoursome variety of tomatoes. If you follow this recipe carefully you will taste bruschetta like you have never tasted it before. I first had it on an archaeological delegation to the Basilicata region of southern Italy. When they brought out the bruschetta I just kept eating it. It was so good I did not really want the main course, much to the amusement of my hosts.

Sliced rustic bread

400 g ripe tomatoes

Extra virgin olive oil

Fresh basil leaves
2 garlic cloves
Salt and pepper

Method

1. Chop the tomatoes into cubes, put in a bowl and sprinkle with salt.
2. Put the tomatoes into a colander set over a bowl. Allow the juices to drain for at least 20 minutes and discard the liquid.
3. Put the drained tomatoes back in a bowl and mix in olive oil, torn fresh basil leaves and one crushed garlic clove.
4. Toast the bread slices. They need to be the size of a French stick cut on the slant.
5. Cut the other garlic clove lengthwise while toasting the bread.
6. Once toasted, rub one side of the bread with the garlic while it is warm.
7. Spoon the tomato mixture on top, grate some fresh black pepper on them – and that's it!

Melon and Prosciutto

Here is another incredibly simple and yet delicious starter from the Mediterranean.

1 honeydew melon (any variety is fine as long as it is ripe)

1 pkt prosciutto

Method

1. Slice the melon, discarding the seeds.
2. Cut the prosciutto slices in half and arrange them on the plate around the melon slices, then serve.
3. Take a piece of melon and wrap a piece of the prosciutto around it, then eat it. Eating the sweet melon with the salty dried ham is a wonderful combination, as well as being one of the healthiest starters.

Mains

Ratatouille

2 onions

2 aubergines

4 courgettes

2 green peppers

2 red peppers

3 garlic cloves

100 ml olive oil

Mixed fresh herbs (rosemary, thyme, oregano, parsley)

250 g ripe, fresh tomatoes

Salt and pepper

Method

1. Chop the onions and garlic and add to a large heavy-based pan with some of the oil and cook until tender.
2. Add the roughly chopped vegetables and the rest of the oil. Cook on a medium heat, stirring all the time, until they begin to soften.

3. Add the herbs and cover and simmer on a low heat for 1 hour.
4. Serve either immediately or cold with cold meats and crusty bread.

Ragu Sauce

The basis of a lot of Italian dishes is a ragu sauce, which could be made into a Bolognese or lasagne. I was told this was how to make a good ragu while working in Italy and was surprised at the addition of the glass of milk, which is used to tenderise the meat and bring out the flavour.

Olive oil for frying
500 g minced beef (not low fat if possible)
2 cloves garlic
1 tsp fresh oregano
2 tbsp tomato purée
1 onion
2 carrots
2 celery sticks
2 × 400 g tins tomatoes (buy Italian if possible)
1 glass wine
1 glass milk
Salt and pepper

Method

1. Put oil in a large heavy-based pan and add chopped onion. Cook until soft.
2. Add the chopped carrot and celery. Cook until tender. Take the vegetables out of the pan and set aside.
3. Add the beef to the hot pan with a little oil and cook until brown, stirring constantly. Then return the vegetables to the pan and mix well.
4. Add the glass of milk and then cover and simmer until most of the milk is absorbed.
5. Add the tomato purée and cook for 1 minute over a hot flame.
6. Add all the other ingredients and bring to the boil, then reduce the heat and simmer gently with a lid on for an hour.
7. You will then have the most delicious and tender sauce you can add to pasta for Bolognese or to make lasagne.

Liver Venezia

The old-fashioned liver and onions of the 1940s and '50s suddenly became fashionable again after people's holidays to Venice, but it is basically the same dish. In the Trentino region of Italy it is served with sliced sautéed potatoes.

450 g onions

450 g lambs liver, thinly sliced

Salt and pepper

45 g plain flour

3 tbsp olive oil

30 g butter

2 tbsp chopped parsley

Method

1. Slice the onions thinly in rings if possible.
2. Trim away any tubes with a knife.
3. Mix the seasoning with the flour and cover the liver with it.
4. Heat oil and butter together until foaming.
5. Add the onions and cook until golden.
6. Add the liver slices and sauté for 3 to 5 minutes on each side until cooked.
7. Stir in the parsley and serve.

Dessert

Olive Oil Apple Cake

360 g plain flour

1 tsp cinnamon

1 tsp bicarbonate of soda

1 tsp baking powder

200 g light brown sugar

2 large eating apples

240 ml olive oil

2 eggs

320 g sultanas

Icing sugar

Juice of a lemon

Method

1. Preheat the oven.
2. Place the peeled, chopped apples in a bowl with the lemon juice and mix them well with the juice.
3. In another bowl, mix the flour, cinnamon, baking powder and bicarbonate of soda.
4. Mix the oil and sugar in a food processor until it lightens in colour.
5. Add the eggs one at a time until well blended.
6. Add the flour and cinnamon and whisk until combined.
7. Transfer the mixture into a large bowl and stir in the apples and sultanas.
8. Line a 9in cake tin with parchment paper and spoon the thick batter into it.
9. Bake in a low oven at for 45 minutes or until a skewer comes out clean.
10. Cool in the pan and dust with icing sugar.

Fresh Fig and Almond Cake

170 g ground almonds

10 fresh figs

Zest and juice of one large lemon

90 g runny honey

60 ml olive oil

2 eggs

Pinch of salt

2 tsp baking powder

½ tsp almond essence

Method

1. Line the base of an 8in cake tin.
2. Mix the honey, olive oil, eggs, salt and lemon juice and zest in a large bowl.
3. Mix the baking powder and ground almonds together, then add to the mixture. Beat until well mixed.
4. Pour the batter into the tin and cut the figs in half lengthwise and lay them over the batter in circles cut side up.
5. Bake for 35 minutes until golden brown and is firm to the touch.
6. Let it cool in the tin, then transfer to a plate and serve with natural yoghurt or single cream.

Christmas Mediterranean

Starter

Watermelon Feta and Mint

This starter is simple but delicious. The sweetness of the watermelon complements the saltiness of the feta perfectly. This is a good dish to serve before rich food

1 watermelon

200 g feta cheese

3 tbs chopped fresh mint

Method

1. Cut the watermelon into small chunks.
2. Cube the feta.
3. Combine the two and sprinkle liberally with fresh mint.
4. Serve in small bowls or cocktail glasses with a sprig of mint on top.

Main

Garlic Slow-Cooked Chicken

By the mid-1980s, garlic was very trendy and viewed as the sign of a sophisticated palate. This recipe is from the south of France. Though simple farmhouse fare, it is a perfect main for a dinner party or unusual Sunday lunch. It takes very little effort, as long as you have a slow cooker or an Aga. It is best served on a large deep platter in the middle of the table so guests can chop pieces of meat off the bird for themselves and spoon the juices onto their plates, to be absorbed by lashings of crusty white French bread. I first discovered this recipe in the 1980s and still make it two or three times a year.

2 kg oven-ready chicken

2 sprigs fresh rosemary

2 sprigs fresh thyme

2 bay leaves

2 tbs olive oil

150 ml white wine

About 40 individual cloves of garlic

French sticks

Method

1. Rub the chicken inside and out with salt and pepper and stuff one sprig of the rosemary and thyme, and one bay leaf into the cavity.
2. Heat the oil until hot in a large frying pan and brown all sides of the chicken.
3. Place the chicken in a slow cooker with the remaining herbs.
4. Pour the wine into the frying pan and stir so it absorbs all the meat juices and burnt chicken. Pour this over the chicken.
5. Add the garlic cloves, unpeeled.
6. Slow cook for about 1 hour on high, then turn the setting down to low and cook for a further 3 hours.

7. This dish will cook perfectly well for another hour, so when the guests arrive you need not take it out of the slow cooker straight away. Once everyone is seated at the table with bowls, spoons, knives and forks, take the chicken out of the cooker and loosely break it up into manageable pieces. Pour over the juices and serve with baskets of sliced French bread. Once you make this dish I am sure that, like me, you will make it many times more.

Dessert

Tiramisu

20 sponge fingers

4 tbsp cold stone black coffee

2 tbsp almond liqueur

4 egg yolks

85 g castor sugar

2 drops vanilla essence

Grated lemon rind

2 tsp lemon juice

350 g mascarpone cheese

20 ml double cream

1 tbsp milk

2 tbsp cocoa powder

1 tbsp icing sugar

Method

1. Arrange the sponge fingers in the base of a serving dish.
2. Put the coffee and liqueur into a bowl and then sprinkle over the sponge fingers.
3. Put the egg yolks into a heatproof bowl with the sugar, vanilla and lemon rind, then stand it over a saucepan of gently simmering water. Whisk until thick and creamy.
4. Put the mascarpone in a separate bowl with the lemon juice and beat until smooth.
5. When the egg mixture is cool, mix it with the mascarpone. Spread half over the coffee-soaked biscuits.
6. Add another layer of biscuits and then top with the remaining mascarpone mixture.
7. Dust the top with cocoa and leave for an hour in the fridge, or better still overnight, before serving.

The 1980s was certainly a decade of contradictions, from hamburgers to nouvelle cuisine, and from mass unemployment to the prosperity enjoyed by yuppies.

In a way, the frugal approach of low-income households during that decade was similar to the recipes from the Second World War, but with the advantage of the microwave oven and freezer. That is, of course, apart from those in British society who were more fortunate and seemed to flourish during the recession. However, it does in a way shine a spotlight on the possible origins of some of the dietary problems we have today. The demonising of fat in our diet in the 1980s is now thought by some medical professionals to have led to the increase in diabetes in the population.

So What is British Food?

WHILE RESEARCHING THIS historic culinary journey, I have found an incredible number of foodstuffs that have been integrated into the British diet from abroad. Although this was primarily due to the culinary influences from around the globe during the dominance of the British Empire, as you have seen, it goes much farther back than that, to the foods brought over to our shores after the Roman invasion. It is strange how much we love spicy food in this country today when our climate produces none of the necessary ingredients. We really took to the spicy foods imported by the Romans from the East, but reverted back to simplistic, plain food during the Saxon and Viking periods. Spicy foods clearly didn't enthuse the Vikings, even though they travelled abroad to just as many places as the Romans. They continued to eat the traditional, plain, high-protein foods that characterise the Scandinavian diet today. Our love of spicy food was renewed after the Crusaders had spent time in the Holy Land.

We seem to have had an amazing ability when confronted with completely alien culinary practices to take them to our hearts and adopt them as our own. Britain really invented fusion food, and we have been doing it for over 2,000 years. No doubt we will continue to do so well into the future.

I thought it was fascinating that the fig and walnut cakes Apicius wrote about in the Roman period were still being made in more or less the same way during the Medieval period. Today, the barbeque represents a link with our prehistoric cooking practices in that it fulfils an ancient desire to cook outdoors. Even though the wood fire was replaced by charcoal (and most recently the gas barbeque), we still love to eat hot meat with our fingers under the stars. Some of my friends tell me that one of the most depressing things about a wet summer is the fact they can't have any barbeques in the evenings. Some even ignore the weather by buying flimsy gazebos so that they can continue their habitual meaty feasts outdoors, no matter what the weather!

Who would have thought that the Romans were making pork and leek sausages 2,000 years ago! It was a real revelation to me when I read Apicius's recipe for those sausages. I thought they were invented in the twenty-first century as a fancy alternative to the normal British sausage, along with venison and pork and apple sausages. In much the same way, the almond-stuffed dates I bought from my local supermarket last Christmas are just a simplified version of the recipe for Dates Alexandrine.

Knowledge of Islamic cooking methods changed our habit of dropping meat into boiling water.

Instead, we now sear it in fat first, and this has really improved the flavour of our gravy. Eating lamb with mint and flavouring our sugar with vanilla pods seems so very British, but these ideas also have their roots in the Middle East. I had always assumed that sweet and sour sauce was a Chinese influence, but that too was in the Baghdad manuscript.

The Medieval type of highly spiced, sweet, yet savoury foods has gone out of favour with us today, but there are still a few long-standing traditions we retain from that period, such as spiced pears in red wine and cherry clafouti/clafoutis, which I have always been led to believe was a nineteenth-century French dish.

The Elizabethans ate syllabub and rice pudding, and the origins of our modern Christmas pudding also came from this period in history, along with the recipe for brandy butter. We see the first recipe for turkey dinner with pigs in blankets (sausages wrapped in bacon) during the seventeenth century, and by the eighteenth century we had added a sage and onion stuffing to our traditional Christmas dinner. We also acquired a love of Welsh Rarebit recipes and toasted cheese in general.

The Georgian period gave us many popular modern recipes: the sandwich and the pork and apple pie to name but a few. The recipe for apple pie with custard inside it was interesting to see, as I had always thought that Mr Kipling invented that! Our Christmas dinners also improved during this period, with the addition of chestnut stuffing, bread sauce, cranberry sauce, gravy and buttered vegetables.

The Victorians, apart from their love of curries, gave us basic kitchen cupboard items such as chutneys and brown, tomato and Worcestershire sauces. They also invented the fondue party that most of us think of as a 1970s' fashion. We still make the Victoria sandwich cake to the same weight of an egg recipe, although we make it into a round cake rather than rectangular fingers.

Recipes from the Second World War have been more or less abandoned by the cooks of Britain today, apart from maybe bubble and squeak, to which we add potatoes. Perhaps this is because wartime cooking was determined by the availability of various foods, rather than our preferences – it is not surprising, therefore, that we don't wish to eat these dishes today. Having said that, dried eggs did enjoy a bit of a revival during the salmonella scare of the late 1980s, and if you look at the recipes included in this section, you will see that, apart from being very economical, many of them were actually very tasty too. Perhaps during these years of the so-called credit crunch, it might be the right time to take another look at them.

The food of the 1970s has made a bit of a comeback lately, as everything retro has suddenly became fashionable. As a result, great recipes like prawn cocktail, duck a l'orange and black forest gateau are being cooked in our kitchens again. The one recipe from the 1970s that is still one of the most popular meals in Britain today is the chicken tikka masala, as a recent *Britain's Best Dish* TV episode demonstrated.

They say that fusion cuisine is the latest thing, and perhaps this is true elsewhere around the globe, but in the case of our small island, fusion cuisine has characterised our cooking practices for hundreds and hundreds of years.

I hope you have enjoyed reading this book – I have certainly enjoyed writing it!

Basic conversion chart

Liquid, Volume

	Imperial	Metric
1/4tsp		1.2 ml
1/2 tsp		2.5 ml
1 tsp		5.0 ml
1/2 tbsp		7.5 ml
1 tbsp	1/2 fl oz	15 ml
1/8 cup	1 fl oz	30 ml
1/4 cup	2 fl oz	60 ml
1/3 cup	2 1/2 fl oz	80 ml
1/2 cup	4 fl oz	120 ml
2/3 cup	5 fl oz	160 ml
3/4 cup	6 fl oz	180 ml
1 cup	8 fl oz	250 ml

Weight

Metric	Imperial	Temperature	
		°F	°C
1/4 oz	7 g	200	90
1/2 oz	15 g	250	120
1 oz	30 g	300	150
2 oz	55 g	350	180
3 oz	85 g	400	200
4 oz (1/4 lb)	115 g	475	250
8 oz (1/2 lb)	225 g		
16 oz (1 lb)	250 g		

Bibliography

Armesto, Felipe Fernandez, Food: A History (London: Macmillan Ltd, 2001)

Beeton, Mrs, Mrs Beeton's Book of Household Management, a first edition facsimile (London: Jonathan Cape Ltd, 1974)

Berriedale-Johnson, Michelle, The British Museum Cook Book (London: British Museum Press, 1987)

Drummond, J.C. and Wilbraham, Anne, The Englishman's Food (London: Pimlico Ltd, 1939)

Flavel, Sidney, Menus and Recipes: Cooking the Flavel Way (London: Sidney Flavel & Co Ltd, 1962)

Glasse, Hanna, The Art of Cookery Made Easy, facsimile edition by Karen Hess (Massachusetts: Applewood Books, 1997)

Isitt, Verity, Take a Buttock of Beef (Southampton: Ashford Press Publishing, 1987)

Mckendry, Maxime, Seven Centuries of English Cooking (London: C. Tinling & Co Ltd, 1973)

Moss, Peter, Meals Through The Ages (London: George G. Harrop Ltd, 1958)

Pegge, Samuel (compiler), The Forme of Cury (Bibliobazaar Ltd, 2006)

Ray, Elizabeth (compiler), The Best of Eliza Acton (Southampton: The Camelot Press Ltd, 1968)

Howells, M., Casseroles and Pies (London, Purnell, 1972)

Latimer, C., Campbell's Clockwatchers Cookbook (London, Esmonde Publishing, 1985)

McWilliam, J., Instant Cooking. (London, Octopus Books Ltd, 1987)

Mulligan, G., Farmhouse Kitchen. (Suffolk, Richard Clay Ltd, 1988)

Newman, R., Cooking for Two. (London, Cathay Books, 1980)

About the Author

Jacqui Wood is best known as *Time Team*'s resident food historian. She works as the Director of Saveock Water Archaeology (www.archaeologyonline.org), an archaeological research centre and field school, and also works for English Heritage demonstrating Bronze Age technology. She lives in Truro.

Index

Also in this series

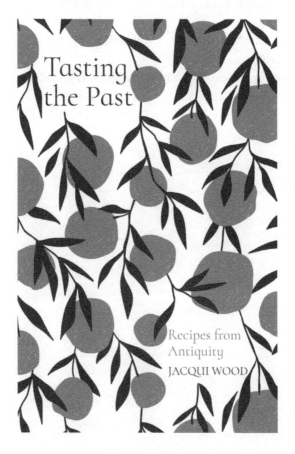

Tasting
the Past

Recipes from
Antiquity
JACQUI WOOD

978 0 7509 9225 1

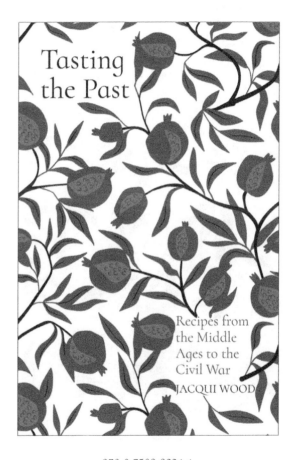

Tasting
the Past

Recipes from
the Middle
Ages to the
Civil War

JACQUI WOOD

978 0 7509 9224 4

Tasting
the Past

Recipes from
George III
to Victoria

JACQUI WOOD

978 0 7509 9223 7

The History Press

The destination for history
www.thehistorypress.co.uk

Method

1. Roast the duck for the required amount of time (see label on the packaging).
2. Transfer to a warm platter and keep hot.
3. Pour on all but 1 tbsp of the fat from the roasting tin (keep the rest of the fat for cooking later).
4. Put the roasting tin over a low heat and stir in the flour.
5. Cook for 2 minutes without browning.
6. Add the orange rind, juice, wine, jelly and sherry and cook gently until the jelly dissolves and the sauce thickens, stirring all the time.
7. Pour over the duck and garnish with orange slices and watercress.

Black Forest Gateau

200 g plain chocolate

2 tbsp milk

200 g unsalted butter

220 g caster sugar

75 g flour

A pinch of salt

4 eggs, separated

Filling

300 ml double cream

225 g black cherry jam or canned cherries, drained

15 g plain chocolate, scraped or grated